LIVING ON WHEELS

LIVING ON WHEELS

by Richard A. Wolters

Illustrated with Photographs and Diagrams

A Sunrise Book

E. P. Dutton & Company, Inc. | New York | 1973

Published simultaneously in Canada
by Clarke, Irwin & Company Limited, Toronto and Vancouver

ISBN: 0-87690-100-3 (cloth)
ISBN: 0-87690-107-0 (paper)
Library of Congress Catalog Card Number: 72–94701

Outerbridge & Lazard, A Subsidiary
of E. P. Dutton & Co., Inc.

CONTENTS

FOREWORD

by Gene Hill
Executive Editor, *Sports Afield*

If anyone can claim to be an expert on Dick Wolters' knowledge of motor homes and campers, I can. I've seen them parked on my lawn and in my driveway for the past ten years.

Dick, to my amazement, took the whole camper thing very seriously right from the start. Here was the ideal way to cadge from his friends without really seeming to do just that. Who notices that the friend in the camper is plugged into your electricity and eating your food? After all, he is in his own home—in your driveway perhaps—but somehow it doesn't seem the same as putting someone up for the weekend.

I always have and always will enjoy Dick's visits, regardless of my personal expenditures. Dick brings qualities to me that no one else ever has: an immense curiosity about things and an equally immense ability to improve on almost everyone else's handiwork—including that of the people who made his wide variety of motor homes and campers.

The avowed purpose of a 'foreword' is to help convince the casual thumber of books to buy. Fine, except that the last person who will read the foreword is the casual thumber. No one reads forewords except the author, who by now is in great need of reassurance. He wants the foreword to nominate him as some sort of contemporary genius. I refuse to do that for Wolters. Instead I will be honest.

Dick is not a genius. He is a serious pragmatist. He is a questioner (of which society can use more); he is perpetually dissatisfied with things as they are—and I'm afraid he is right. Dick is the kind of guy who wears two watches and keeps asking you what time it is.

No matter how good something is, I honestly believe that Wolters can, more often than not, make it better or easier. Or stronger, or whatever it should really be. Dick is by nature a tinkerer, in the finest sense of the word. He has that rare eye for the third dimension of space and movement. He can look at something and really *see* what makes it work. I cannot. That's why I let him use my electricity, water and whiskey.

This book, which I know very, very well, is filled with ideas, hints, tips and suggestions that are of that rare breed of being obvious, full of common sense and absolutely right—once someone else has pointed them out to you. The world is full of simple explanations that are obvious once someone has explained them to us: gravity, the telephone, the safety pin and the zipper.

Dick thinks it's fun to improve on someone else's thinking. And I think he's right . . . in more ways than one. I will also admit that Wolters can be insufferable when he pinpoints a simple solution to a problem that's been bothering someone else for quite a while. My first reaction is just like yours: "Why didn't I think of that?" But what little honesty I have left compels me to admit that I never would have. I would have bought this book, except I have a free copy and also Wolters himself—still plugging into my outside receptacle.

Someone has recently written that so long as our society looks down on plumbers because their work is ignoble and flatters poor philosophers because their calling is noble, we shall have neither good plumbers nor good philosophy. Neither our piping nor our ideas will hold water.

This is a book written by a fine plumber who rightly believes that it's better to know how to fix it than be content to be philosophical when your icebox won't make ice.

May 1973 G. H.

PART I
IN THE BEGINNING

If there is a place called Disasterville, that's where I've always managed to pitch my tents. My earliest memory of camping under
canvas concerns Treasure Island in the Delaware River, to which I
traveled with Boy Scout Troup No. 12. All that seems to have
stayed with me is the recollection of cold food, a storm that flooded
our tent, and a terrible desire to be home. I was only ten, the
mascot of the troop, and it was ten more years before I dared set
foot in a tent again.

Then in college someone suggested a weekend of camping. It sounded like a lark, but it, too, ended with our camp being soaked and once again a desire to be back in my own warm bed.

Again, just after World War II, two of us were dropped off by boat on an uninhabited Pacific island off the Bikini atoll. We were on a scientific mission to photograph the bird life. When we beached our rubber raft and unloaded our supplies, I remember kissing the sand. It was the first I'd been on solid ground for over a month. We set up camp for our overnight stay. I enjoyed every moment of that experience until a vicious tropical storm inundated our tent; and solid ground or not, I wanted to be back in my dry sack on board ship.

After that, ten more years went by, but I still hadn't learned enough to stay away from tents permanently. The next mistake took place above the Arctic Circle. I landed on Baffin Island late one night, only to discover that there wasn't a bed to be had within a thousand miles. A canvas tied to the plane with a sleeping bag under it was home. It was to be my first tent experience without rain . . . it snowed. The desire for a warm bed was urgent. The next and last episode was on a fishing trip. Three of us city fellows went to the Green Mountains to fish for their famous trout. This time I had learned my lesson. It was a starlit night, and my companions laughed at me as I set up a tarpaulin over my sleeping bag. I tied two corners to a rail fence, the third to a sapling, and the fourth to the rear bumper of our jeep. When the rains did come, I had it made. My poor companions who wanted to sleep under the stars didn't fare so well. They woke me during the height of the storm and asked if I wanted to go find a motel; their sleeping bags were soaked. I realized my refusal was a mistake the moment they drove off down the road . . . with my "roof" tied to their bumper.

With that background, I now start this book. Don't be disheartened. Although my credentials for living under canvas aren't too impressive, you can understand that these same credentials make me an expert in seeking out comfort. A man sitting on a wet log drinking his evening martini is only half civilized.

There had to be a better way without abandoning the out-of-doors. While I mulled the thought around in my head, two other

2

things were happening. First, in the mail came a fat check for a fishing story I had done on assignment for one of the national magazines. Second, it was a rainy Sunday morning and my wife was reading *The New York Times*. Nothing escaped her eye. Even the print was weary by time she got through with it. She clipped something out, a trait from her mother's side, and handed it to me.

> VOLKSWAGEN CAMPER. Sleeps 2 adults and 2 children, bottle gas stove, heater, refrigerator, hanging tent. . . .

It's hard to remember if I said, "Let's go!" before or after my hat was on.

My wife, Olive, wanted to change her clothes. I said "No."

She wanted to do her hair. I said "No."

She wanted me to drive slower. I said "No."

All this saying "No" is not really in character, but from the moment I saw the first line of the ad I envisioned arriving and the seller saying, "You should have been here five minutes ago."

The address was the TWA parking lot at Idlewild Airport. That was in the days before the jet. I made it . . . at jet speed.

Airline Captain Jackson, uniform and all, stood leaning against a two-tone blue VW bus converted into a camper. He was a cinch to spot that Sunday morning at the other end of the deserted airport parking lot. I gunned the motor to be first across the line.

A DOLL HOUSE ON WHEELS

We were the first to arrive in answer to the ad. We looked, we touched, we smiled, and we were only half-listening to the sales pitch. Captain Jackson didn't seem to know that I'd bought it before I'd arrived. It was a doll house on wheels. We'd never seen anything like it.

The captain, who had been stationed in Germany, had used the VW camper for exploring Europe. He told us of his trips there and how much he enjoyed this new way of traveling. He went on to explain that we could practically live in this unit without depending on any outside conveniences. We would be self-contained. Then he showed us how it all worked. The wide entrance doorway on the curb side, toward the back, had two swinging doors. On their backs were folding shelves and storage spaces for canned food. Inside the doorway there was a cabinet on top of which was a small sink with a galley pump. Inside that cabinet was a single-burner gas stove. Ingenious! On the other side of the doorway a clothes closet hung against the wall. The two back seats faced each other, with a table between them. That was the dinette. It all folded down and became the bed . . . for two people who didn't mind close quarters. Under one of the seats was the water tank. Under the other seat was a gasoline heater that would keep the place warm in a blizzard. The roof had a hinged trap door so you could stand up in that area. Cute curtains all around gave you privacy at night. There was a roof rack for storage and a tent to hang on the side of the bus that gave you an extra room. The front seat became the second bed. It was as though the captain were performing a magic act for my delighted wife. And a showman he was . . . when he opened the two-cubic-foot refrigerator I just had to giggle. What a toy!

Up drove a car. A dejected looking man got out and said one word: "Sold?"

"Yep," I answered.

"Want to make a fast hundred?"

"Nope."

He drove off.

In a few minutes I was driving my new house home. Olive followed in our car. A couple of miles down the road I pulled off to the side. She stopped behind me. "What's the matter?" she called.

"Where's the motor?" I asked. I hadn't even looked at it.

This is what the men on Madison Avenue call impulse buying. I just wanted that "thing." I had no idea what it was all about or that it was going to change my whole life-style.

When we arrived at home, it took no time at all for my neighbors to gather around to see the eighth wonder of the world. As the crowd gathered, new arrivals were given a complete demonstration.

"Show 'em the bed," came from the audience.

"The stove," called another.

4

"Don't forget the refrigerator."

Our neighbors were as excited as we were. The fun began when one of the men suggested we try to put up the tent. One bag on the roof rack held the pipes and one the canvas. A whoop went up from the crowd when we opened the tent bag. It was not an ordinary brown or green; it was orange and green, with blue stripes.

It took a half-hour to figure out how the tent hung onto the bus. It was a funny-looking thing, like an awkward puppy . . . you just had to love it. The show ended with a party. Frank from down the street brought a gallon of wine and some glasses. "Let's christen it," he said as he started to pour.

If I had thought at that time that I'd someday be writing a book on this whole thing I'd have kept all sorts of notes and anecdotes. But it's really better this way. I look back at that period with the funny-looking VW bug as one remembers his first girl friend in junior high school.

I'll always remember our first camping trip. We parked on the bank of the Beaverkill River. The fishing was excellent, and the one-burner stove did a magnificent job of sautéeing trout. The meal was leisurely and quiet; the kids were playing down by the river as Olive and I had our coffee. There was a peace and comfort about the setting that I tried to put into words . . . but it didn't work. How does one tell his wife that this moment is what the whole game is all about? I never said it because like a mother bear she put her nose up to catch the breeze that came through the VW's open door. "I'd better get the kids. It's going to rain."

Secretly I hoped it would. We rushed to get settled for the night.

To do the dishes we had to stand outside and work in the opening of the big side doors. We heated water on the stove. The tent that hung over the open doorway would protect us even if the rain came before we finished. I kept an eye on the approaching storm and half-muttered, "Come on, baby, rain."

What a pleasant feeling it was to be warm in a snug bed with the rain pelting on the metal roof. It took me forty years to learn that trick.

There were a lot of other tricks I had to learn. Possibly they didn't have mosquitoes in Germany where they made our VW, but we were eaten alive on our first trip to Vermont. My resourceful wife had the answer. We went to work on yards and yards of mosquito netting. Magnets were sewn into the edges of the fabric; then when we stopped to set up our overnight address, all doors and windows were covered.

As the fall approached we faced another problem. Beau, our English setter and member of the family, ended his day's hunting wet and dirty. He was making a shambles of the interior. Solution: we cut a wire kennel, like the one he had at home, down to size and placed it just inside the rear door. He'd sit happily for hours watching the traffic out the back window. When Tar, our Labrador retriever, came along he was trained to sleep and stay with Beau. It was close quarters, but the dogs were no different from the people . . . it was tight living. In the winter when all the doors were closed and the heater kept us snug, we had to dress one at a time. A Buckingham Palace it wasn't.

The summer and fall were a delight. We were off every weekend. At twenty miles per gallon and no motel bills, we could afford to be a very active family. As winter approached we already knew how we were going to spend it. The camper called for some customizing. I started on a kitchen box. It turned out to be an ingenious Rube Goldberg affair—14″ × 16″ × 18″. It held everything for the kitchen: pots, pans, utensils, condiments, also the dishes and silverware. It had drawers, slots, hooks, shelves; it swung open, out, and over on hinges. It wouldn't have won an industrial design award, but I've since learned if it had, it wouldn't have worked as well. It was made to fit under the seat next to the water tank . . . well, that is, the *new* water tank. The five-gallon tank that came with the unit wasn't much more than drinking water for the dogs. I pulled it out and built a twelve-gallon tank out of a new material called Fiberglas. Twelve whole gallons . . . we were in clover. A collapsible canvas bucket supplemented our camping needs . . . in those days stream water could be used for washing.

The big winter project was a new tent. The one that came with the unit was an awkward affair. It was made of very heavy canvas and hung from a frame that attached to the roof. We needed something with a floor and screening, so Olive designed it and then made

6

it on her sewing machine. This was nothing new for her to tackle; when we had an eighteen-foot sailboat she made the sails to save money. The sailcloth cost only $36. That saved us about $114 on the sails. Of course, it was too big a job for her home sewing machine and it cost me $300 back in those days to buy a new one. I can't tell you how much the tents cost to make because it gets too

What started out as simple camping became an apartment in the woods. Try taking this "house" down in the rain . . . but in good weather it was great!

complicated figuring out the price of having the new sewing machine rebuilt. But we ended up with not just one tent but a series of tents. We had a wing for cooking. Zippered to that was a screened-in wall tent with a plastic-coated nylon floor. All four sides of that tent had zippered-in storm covers. Zippered to that tent was a roofed-over patio area. I had a fortune invested in nine-foot zippers. The whole complex weighed less than our original striped tent. We added a folding table for cooking, a two-burner gasoline stove, chairs that folded up like umbrellas, and a lot of camping gadgets.

When we were ready to roll in the spring I started to wonder how that little twenty-eight-horsepower engine was going to get us up the first hill . . . and one day it decided not to. We replaced it with a new forty-horse engine and off we went to Maine.

Tar, our Labrador, was fast becoming an outstanding field-trial dog, and Bud Leavitt of Bangor, Maine, asked if I'd bring him up for his TV show. We drove up and set up camp outside of Bangor. When Bud arrived where we were camped he almost doubled over with laughter.

"You city people are trying to turn our woods into suburbia," he said. He was so impressed with the comforts of life that we had established for ourselves that he asked us to break down camp, pack it up, and set it up again for his TV cameras.

A NEW WAY

A whole new way of life was unfolding. I'm not sure if I recognized when it started to happen, but it happened and that's the important thing. When we acquired the little house on wheels we were very much a trout-fishing family. Many years ago I wrote a book called *Beau*. It was the story of how I became interested in dogs and upland game hunting. With all the characters in the book, a great dog and some wonderful men, I neglected to give the little camper its due credit for making all of this possible. I just couldn't have traveled as much if I'd had to do it using motels. After all, those were the years when we were building a family and home and we

8

couldn't spend *all* our money on the fun things.

I finally realized it when one of my neighbors said something about it to me. It was one of those rare weekends when I was home raking the leaves. He leaned on his rake and said to me, "I sure envy all the things you do. Wish I had the money to do it."

I tried to point out to him that it wasn't money that made it possible, it was the camper that did it. He had a second car and could afford it. Our second car was the VW bus, and twenty miles per gallon was a cheap way to go. The food costs were the same whether we ate at home or in camp. The difference was the fun, and I never considered playing nursemaid to a lawn fun, nor for that matter, raking leaves. He scratched his head and muttered something about wondering how his wife Betty would take to that idea.

By now Tar had developed into a fine working dog. He was so good that he became a hero in our family. We recognized his talent at a very young age and took him to a field trial to test his hunting ability against other fine retrievers. He loved it and so did we. Before we even knew what was happening, the little blue house was steering us around the countryside on the field-trial circuit. Every weekend we were off campaigning our dog. From Maine to Virginia we traveled the circuit. Many of the other dogs were owned by very rich men. How could I compete with that? Tar didn't mind a bit how much money his competitors had; he put me in their league and the VW made the traveling possible. Thursday night after work the clothes would be packed and the food put into the two-cubic-foot refrigerator. Friday night we'd be on the road as soon as I got in the door from work. This would never have happened if I'd had to make motel reservations in advance. That's not my style, and besides I couldn't have afforded that route. So credit has to be given to the mobility that our camper gave us. A book, *Water Dog,* came out of that experience. This was book number three. None of them would have been published if I'd stayed home tending a flower bed.

As I look back over those years when we had the little camper, I half-remember thinking at the time about the things that were not

We added the little white one . . . now we were a complete tent city.

exactly right with it. But I don't remember expressing it; one doesn't tell family secrets in public. Actually, at that time, it was the best thing of its kind. It was very unusual to own such a vehicle then, so how could I be disloyal?

Truly, it was like puppy love with one's first girl. But puppy love is fickle. In truth, at times she was a little bit of a pain in the neck. Slowly the realization came to me while we were on a vacation in Canada that the little blue bus converted to a house was not the right "girl friend" for me. The outside tent was a real problem. I was proud of it and gave my good wife all the credit she deserved for being so clever. But a tent is a tent and putting it up and taking it down with two straight weeks of rain got past the fun stage. Although Olive and I weren't sleeping in the tent, the kids were. Our daughter had graduated from the front seat "bed" because she had started to grow. The story can best be summed up by saying that being caught in a hurricane in Nova Scotia was a mess.

There was another thing that started to get to me. The new super highways were springing up all over the countryside. Everyone was now traveling at sixty and seventy miles per hour. Our little bus with a forty-horsepower engine could give us a good fast forty-eight miles per hour if I really pushed her. It wasn't the VW's fault . . . not the way we had her loaded down. But the only vehicles I ever passed were the highway department mowing machines or cars that had a breakdown. I didn't have too much to say about it at the time because we were all really attached to our little blue house on wheels. It takes time to switch girl friends; but when it happens, it can happen fast.

10

By this time a lot of people were moving around the country on wheels. Trailers had become very popular. A new vehicle was being developed on the West Coast; it was called a pick-up camper. It was actually a trailer built on top of a pick-up truck. A writer friend from New Mexico drove one East. He called from Pittsburgh.

"I'm going to be in New York for a few days. I'm driving a camper and wonder if you could let me park it on your place."

I'd seen a couple of these new vehicles on the road and a few pictures in magazines, but here was an opportunity to see one up close.

He quickly added, "You can use it if you like. It's really something!"

When Walt drove into our back yard the next night I was amazed to see how big his camper looked next to our VW. When Olive stepped into it the same expression came on her face as she had worn when Captain Jackson showed us the little blue camper many years before. I had an idea Walt's phone call was going to cost me a lot of money, but at least I'd save the frustration of putting up and taking down tents.

We didn't get to take a trip in Walt's camper, but we did examine and study it closely. There was no question about it. We were going to move up. We were going to "high school" and were about to get a new "girl friend." This time we would have a better idea of what we'd need.

While we still had Walt's camper in our back yard we took all its measurements. We sat in it during the evenings and tried to figure out how we would live in such a vehicle. We mentally went through the motions of living in it. Where would things be stored? How would we dress, cook, sleep, and just relax? We even tried it out one night—the whole family slept in it, right in the back yard.

With all the measurements in hand, we set about to make a cardboard mock-up of the floor plan to scale. The little blue camper had taught us a lot—some things we wanted to change because of the way we lived and some things the manufacturer had overlooked in his design.

11

First we needed a good-sized dog kennel. It had to have its own outside door. There was no need to bring wet dogs into the house; any camper was too small for that. The kennel could occupy the space under one of the seats. It would be a king-sized house for the dogs. On the inside the kennel should have a large wire door so the dogs could always see and smell us and feel, in spite of their quarters, that they were still part of the family. The inside door would allow us to let them in with us when we wanted. This arrangement would make everybody happy—dogs love a secure cave.

The floor in our first camper was very cold in the winter, so we figured out a way to have a false floor with an air space built in. This floor was to be laid in sections and each section could be raised on hinges. A rug would go over it, but the space between the floors would make an excellent area to store heavy items like shotguns, ammunition, canned food, and tools. The storage space would also act as insulation.

The galley in the camper was sensational. There was no way to improve it. A three-burner stove with an oven was a real step up. The Fiberglas counter and sink gave the cook plenty of work space. The refrigerator was four cubic feet, a luxury.

We tried all the appliances. The bottled-gas furnace threw out a lot of heat, but we noticed that the warmth rose to the ceiling. Somehow we had to get the air circulating. I knew I could install a rubber-bladed fan to do the job. That made us think about the electrical wiring. It was all within the wall. We marked our plan to show the manufacturer where we wanted extra outlets. Lighting was not adequate in the camper. We wanted lights in the closets and a better reading lamp. I could put the lights in if the wiring was installed before the walls were closed in.

Without having had experience with the little camper, I would have never questioned some of the design decisions the manufacturer made, but I saw two problems. The unit carried only one bottle of LP gas for cooking, refrigeration, and heating; we wanted two. We'd had an experience in the back country in Maine the previous summer that dictated this change. We'd spent all morning driving on logging roads to a stream. When we got there we set up camp and then discovered we'd run out of gas for the refrigerator. We had to drive all the way back to civilization, losing a whole day.

Since you can't tell how full the bottle of gas is, we wanted a second bottle installed . . . a full one always ready to go. The solution here was simple. The manufacturer installed one bottle, in its metal compartment, lying on its side. We made the measurements and discovered that two compartments could be installed in the same area if they were stood up. The way it worked out solved another problem. They had a fifteen-gallon fresh water storage tank next to the bottled gas. That was not going to be enough water. With the new arrangement we were able to get a twenty-five-gallon tank in.

Olive raised a very interesting point one evening while we were sitting in Walt's unit. She said, "You know, what we'd been doing in the blue camper was half-camping. With a pick-up camper there will be no camping: we'll live inside this one . . . what problems does it raise?"

One was privacy. We figured out a curtain arrangement that we could install ourselves. That settled that problem. Then we thought about having guests in. People like to smoke when they drink or eat. Since Olive was allergic to cigarette smoke we knew that she'd have a problem in such a small area. The solution was a ceiling vent fan. I'm so glad that we had enough sense to sit and think of all these details before we ordered our camper. That fan was worth a hundred times what it cost.

By playing with the cardboard floor plan (we had the measurements of the closets, doorway, beds, cabinets, etc.) Olive figured a way to get two extra ceiling wall cabinets installed. She discovered some other things, too. There was wasted space in the closets. Her plan called for shelves near the floor. Also, all cabinets had to have divider shelves or the space near the top would be wasted. I'd never have thought about these things. My clear-sighted wife wasn't awed by the appliances and the decor. She went to the heart of things.

There were two more problems that took a lot of time to figure out. Secretly I missed my morning shower when we went off in the VW camper. I never mentioned it to anyone because I just wasn't going to admit that anything was wrong with our way of living on the road. I'm not so sure how well I kept my secret after being out for a few days. Although the new pick-up campers had the luxury of a toilet, it would be a few years before the industry would figure out how to install a shower. We worked that problem out before they did. We made a shower stall out of vinyl plastic—a big plastic bag that hung from the ceiling with boat snaps. A doorway was cut into the side of the bag. From the inside a larger piece of plastic was closed over the door so it was watertight. The bottom of the bag was on the floor. We attached a hose to the corner of the bag at the floor and that was the drain. We drilled a hole in the floor of the camper and put the hose through it. We installed a boat drain in the camper floor. A metal plate covered the hole when it wasn't in use. The shower itself was fashioned out of our collapsible canvas bucket that hung from the ceiling. A three-foot hose was connected to the bottom of the bucket along with a shut-off valve. A small sprinkler head was attached to the end of the hose and it worked down to the last drop.

As simple as it was, the shower inspired some pretty good singing. Three showers could be taken with one filling. A tea kettle of boiling water mixed in with a full bucket of water from the nearest stream made the temperature just right. It turned out to be a real fun thing . . . a conversation piece. It all folded down to the size of a rolled-up pair of pants. The only problem was that it was a major project to set it up. Shower time on the road turned into one of those old-fashioned Saturday night affairs. Everybody had to shower . . . not so much to save water as to save time converting the house into a shower and dressing room. Surprisingly enough, in all the years we used the shower, it never ripped; although we carried repair materials just in case. On many occasions we dressed for formal affairs in our camper. Try that in a tent.

There was one problem with the new pick-up campers that I didn't like: the cab was completely separate from the living quarters. In our VW camper we were all together, I might even say, packed together; but in this unit the driver would be isolated. I asked Walt, one of the evenings he was with us, how he felt about it. He told this story. He and his wife were on a long trip out West. After driving many hours he got tired, and she relieved him at the wheel. They pulled over to the side of the road, and she went around to the driver's side. He decided to go in the back and take a nap on one of the beds. Why sleep sitting up, he might as well do it in style. After a time she stopped for gas and decided to use the ladies' room. He woke up, saw where they were, and decided to use the men's room in the station. When he came out she was gone. A hundred miles later she discovered he'd "left her."

Walt and I talked this problem over. I didn't like the isolation. If I wanted a simple thing like a Coke, I'd have to stop, get out, walk around the vehicle, open the door, and get into the camper to get it. With the VW camper I was used to having a sandwich made for me while I was driving down the road. If I wanted a glass of milk someone could get it for me without my having to stop; besides, it's no fun being separated from the people you're traveling with. What could we do about it? Before the night was out we came up with two solutions. The first one was five years ahead of its time. If we cut the back out of the cab, cut a hole in the camper, and ordered the pick-up truck with bucket seats we could walk between them and into the back. Walt thought it was a great idea but said we'd never get a pick-up truck with bucket seats. We all settled for the second solution. Why not take out the rear window in the cab, cut a hole in the living quarters, and make it a crawl-through between the cab and the camper? It could all be weather-proofed. The driver could talk to people in the back, have his food handed up, and it would be big enough for even Daddy to crawl back and forth.

TRADING UP AND FIXING UP

We were ready to fire a letter off to Kansas and see if the company would make our unit. We never got a return letter; instead they called us on the phone. They were very excited with our ideas, especially the one about the pass-through. I'm not saying that we had this idea first, but it became optional on units sold by this company the following year. Soon every company had it, and some years later the walk-through was available, bucket seats and all.

When our new camper arrived it was the latest thing of its kind on the road. The whole family was excited, but we really felt bad when the man came to buy our little blue VW camper. Although I was glad to see the tents go, it was like losing an old friend.

Even the dogs liked the new kennel on wheels. It was so spacious; the decor was so modern. Once we learned to live in it, life became easy. We spent every weekend away and also started to plan our first cross-country trip.

We thought we knew it all when we ordered the new unit, but we soon found out that we still had much to learn . . . and that's what this book is all about. We learned some other things too. Not only didn't we know as much as we thought, but a lot of people in the business didn't have the answers either . . . and that's what this book is about too!

With all our experience and with all the planning with the scaled mock-up, we still found areas to install five more storage cabinets. Wasted space, living on wheels, is a kind of crime. This might not sound too important, but we had four people, two adults and two kids, and two dogs living in a house ten feet long and seven feet wide. Every inch of space had to count. Although we thought the kitchen galley was impossible to improve upon, we managed a half-dozen things to make life easier for the cook. Remember how we sat in the camper and played the role of living in it? We forgot a number of things. Where was the mirror to shave by? Where would I plug in my electric razor? What about a shaving light? What about a long mirror for Olive to use for dressing? Where would we store the bedding during the day? One by one we solved all these and many more questions.

Did you ever try to take off your shoes while leaning against a wall? That's what we discovered we had to do once the bed was down for the night. Since the seats converted into the bed, it left us no place to sit. We solved that one by building a folding bench against the wall. I got the idea while riding an elevator and seeing the operator pull a folding bench down from against the wall.

16

When we ordered the truck on which our camper body was going to be built, our local dealer had us contact the truck division of his company. He didn't know the requirements for campers since he'd never seen one. I was getting one of the first ones in the state. We talked by phone to the vice president of the recreation vehicle department. He assured me that they knew all about campers. He cited the fact that out West these units were very popular and his engineers had made a complete study of the needs. Yes, they knew what kind of springs to build in, how to set up the battery and its size. Yes, they'd get the right tires on it. As for motor size, that was my choice. I chose the biggest in their line.

The vice president proved to be wrong on every count. The way it turned out, my decision on the engine was the only correct one.

Wheels on wheels and not a tent to be seen . . . real luxury.

We had to have extra springs built into the chassis. A second battery had to be put in. The way they had it set up, one battery operated the motor and the house lights in the camper. One cold night I sat up reading late; I awoke the next morning to discover that we had a dead battery. I installed a second one myself.

The company engineer's decision on tires was a disaster. We had a blowout in the first hundred miles. Luckily we rolled into a station and replaced the tire. The second blowout was four thousand miles later in the Badlands of South Dakota. This time we weren't so lucky. We were thirty miles from the nearest town. I got the spare out and went to work. With the jack that was provided by the engineers, I started to lift the axle off the ground. The jack gears stripped. They had provided a toy to do a man's job. This was not funny in the middle of the Badlands in July. We waited half a day for a car to come along and take us to town for a hydraulic jack.

Next day, when we finally got to a city, I replaced all the tires. The ones that came with our vehicle were not big enough to handle our load. It wasn't a bill of goods the local salesman was giving to an out of stater. He showed me the tire-weight load table in his book. It was episodes like this that shook my confidence in the "experts."

We named the new camper "Lablover's Landlubber." Landlubber because she looked like a ship and was as functional and compact as any quarters below deck . . . but she only sailed on land. Lablover because we fell in love with the Labrador retriever breed, and Tar was doing so well. We were the envy of our field-trial club. The camper became the "field office" at the trials, especially on cold days. Instead of feeding the judges a cold sandwich during the lunch break, we'd have them in for a hot meal. It didn't take us very long to find out the real advantages of the camper. We could entertain in it if the weather was bad or sit outside in beach chairs if the day was clear. It was so spacious compared to our first one that living in it was fun.

All spring we followed the field-trial circuit. Tar was winning a lot of ribbons, and between time we added little refinements to the interior of the camper to make life easier on the road. They were little things, almost too insignificant to mention, but they proved to be important. We had stood the fishing rods, in their cases, in the back of the closet. We soon found that every time we opened the closet door, after we'd been traveling, the rod cases fell out. We fixed that by drilling holes in the rear of the shelf near the floor and slipping each case into its slot. Sugar and salt could never be found when we wanted them, so we built a holder and hung it out of the way but within arm's reach of the table. The cabinets in the galley needed organization: compartments were made, drawers were organized with dividers. Towel racks and soap trays were added to what came with the unit. I installed an extra fire extinguisher near the door, and I was glad I did.

One day I stopped at a gas station to get the oil changed. The attendant interrupted repairs he was making on a car to do our job. When he finished with us he went back to his other work. I turned to call good-bye as I opened the door of the camper to get the kids in. The attendant came running out of the station! I was stunned! He was enveloped in flames. Automatically I reached for the fire extinguisher at the door. I can't even remember pointing it or covering him with the foam, but the flames were out before they got to his body. He was shaken badly, but happy. This is a dramatic way of proving that everything has to have its place and be in place in this kind of living.

By summer we had worked all the kinks out of our unit and were ready to cross the country. Although this was fast becoming the way of life in the West, as yet we still weren't seeing many campers in the East. Our neighbors were concerned about where we would stay each night. Our attitude was, we'll just go and see.

Our plan was simple. We'd drive as fast as we could to the Mississippi River and from there on we'd go at our own pace. The only commitments we made were some field trials; we'd try our luck with Tar.

When we returned home from this trip we were surprised to find that our neighbors and friends seemed to be more interested in where we stayed and our role as nomads than the sights we had seen. People don't seem to ask where you have been as often as where did you stay.

Many of the sights we saw are very hazy in my memory, but not the places where we stayed. This interest and my own strong memories of those places seem to indicate that there is something innate in man about the importance of where he settles and rests. Possibly it's something that has come down through our genes and has to do with safety and self-preservation.

The first stop on that trip was in Ohio. We visited some friends and stayed on their property for the weekend to run Tar in a field trial. He won a ribbon there, and we were very pleased as we headed west for the Mississippi. The trip didn't really start for me until we had the river in view. Up until then it was much the same as an ordinary weekend trip for us. Possibly what made the difference was the excitement the kids showed on seeing "Ole Man" river, or my realization that we were now on our own.

It had been a long drive to La Crosse, Wisconsin, and we arrived just before supper. When we crossed a bridge I noticed a sign with directions to a park on the river. I turned in, thinking it would be fun to eat supper by the river and the kids could go wading. It turned out to be so delightful that we changed our plan and stayed a full day. The river was clean and the countryside was peaceful. We were parked only a stone's throw from the water on the edge of a grove of trees. I remember that there was no charge for staying in this little park. It was something the town provided for travelers, as well as a weekend recreation area for their own people. Having only been away from New York a few days, I guess this friendly attitude impressed me.

The first stop on the west bank of the great river was typical of our six-week trip. One night we arrived very late in a small town near Mitchell, South Dakota, and I was very tired. We didn't know where to stay so I stopped and asked a policeman in a patrol car where we could spend the night. He said, "Follow me." Laughingly, my wife suggested that he might be taking us to jail.

He took us off the main road about a quarter of a mile and pointed out an area to stay. Next morning we were delighted to discover we were in a wonderful camp site. It had a pond, a play area for small children, and a shelter for bad weather. It was clean, and picnic tables were all around. It was all very attractive. I spotted a sign on a post:

> If you have traveled a long way to get here, we hope you have had a good rest. When you go on, we hope you'll remember us as nice folks.

The Elks Club

Even if our stay was only to be overnight, we played a game every morning before we left any area. It was called "pick-up." It was a way of being sure that we left a camp site cleaner than we'd found it.

On the days when we wanted to cover a lot of ground, we'd start early, only stopping to eat and refuel. Our longest layover would be for supper. That way the driver could get a good rest and be able to drive on into the evening. When we got tired we'd either stay in a roadside rest area (though local ordinances ban this in certain areas) or we'd ask a gasoline attendant if we could park behind the station. We tried the state parks for overnight accommodations on one occasion. We arrived late, only to discover that they were so crowded that we could not even get in the gate. We were charged three dollars anyway to register and have the privilege of parking outside in a clearing by the road. Needless to say, we didn't try that again.

We came to enjoy the freedom we were having, moving and staying when and where we pleased. Our visit for about five days in Wyoming was typical of the rest of the trip. We saw a stream paralleling the main highway. It was very pretty, and it looked as though it held trout. We turned off onto the first side road and explored the area. A dirt road led us to our stream. We finally found a flat clearing and that became our home for the next three days. We never saw a car or another person the whole time we were there. We spent the days fishing and walking. It was a quiet, peaceful time, but we noticed that the kids became restless. We moved on.

Heading for Coty, we rolled into a private campground there. It offered everything we needed. Washers and dryers were available, and the hot showers were a joy. The local lumber yard helped me build a new wooden chock to replace one that had broken. We enjoyed the change of pace, three days alone and then a few days with swarms of kids and adults around. This was what our children needed. They had been cooped up too long. Groups were organized to go to the rodeo at night, and museums were visited in the afternoons. The swimming pool was where the young people had fun and where the adults made friends.

This taught us a lot about the social life on wheels. People relaxed the barriers. After a ten- or fifteen-minute chat at the laundromat or at the pool, it's perfectly acceptable to invite someone to stop over for a drink before dinner. It seemed easier for people to make friends in their homes away from home. Possibly people extend their friendship because they know that the relationship is transient. Whatever the reason, it makes traveling this way enjoyable.

In Montana we had another experience I remember vividly. At Livingston we stopped at the fishing tackle shop, bought a few supplies, and asked about the streams in the area. The proprietor was extremely helpful. He gave me his card and suggested that I drive out to a ranch and ask if we could fish and stay on their land.

This seemed like a terrible imposition, and Olive didn't like the idea at first. We talked it over and decided we'd try. The ranch was a magnificent place situated in a valley about twenty miles outside of town. The rancher couldn't have been nicer. He drove with us about five miles back into his property and showed us a spot on the small river that looked like a calendar picture. It was the best fishing I'd ever had in my life, and I've fished halfway around the world. The sheer beauty of the valley was worth the trip West.

The concern our neighbors and friends back home had expressed about where we would stay was proving groundless. With a little ingenuity we were finding garden spots on our own. We had planned to see a number of the national parks on our trip. We did so, but our stays in these parks were cut short because they were overcrowded. We saw the sights and then went off for one of our own side trips. For example, the wildlife in Yellowstone Park seemed rigged. But, from the roof of our camper, only fifty miles from Yellowstone, we watched elk, moose, and bears in their natural environment, without hordes of people around. We stayed there that night. Once again, after the experience of the park, we enjoyed being alone.

The next morning we discovered that we weren't as alone as we had thought. Through the night the bears had come within feet of our camper. The kids were fascinated by the paw prints. We discovered we had some other visitors; two campers had come into the clearing to join us. They carried two families from Seattle. We had some morning coffee together and they suggested we all travel together. The kids, especially mine, thought it was a great idea.

Both campers from Seattle had bright yellow motorcycles on racks attached to their back bumpers. It didn't take long for our children to tell me the advantages of these low-powered trail bikes. They were excellent for cross-country trips; they could go up and over a mountain; and they were safe for kids to ride off highways. The advantage that I saw was that they would give us mobility without moving the whole rig. To go to town for a quart of milk in the big camper was foolish. A motor bike would have saved us a lot of trouble when we had the blowout and a useless jack in the Badlands of South Dakota. So I talked myself into buying a bright yellow trail bike.

We had a lot of fun for the next week with our friends from Seattle. We camped wagon-fashion for a few days at Glacier National Park, but the parts I remember best were the side trips back into country that it would have taken days to cover on foot. Even with the kids on the jump seat, the trail bikes covered a lot of territory. The little bikes became our work horses. Groceries were no longer a chore—the kids begged to go; they wrote letters so we could find the nearest post office. Even the dogs liked the bikes. They'd run alongside for miles and get some good exercise. On a couple of occasions I took trips back into the mountains to find virgin trout water while the family went off to town to spend the

This was the way to see Montana, or any place . . . a new life-style.

day. A whole new world opened up.

The last day in Montana I went off for one more day of mountain fishing. Olive went into town to do some last-minute buying and we rendezvoused on the road in late afternoon. We were off to Jackson Hole, Wyoming. We had promised the kids we'd return to Wyoming and take them to see the pageant depicting the reenactment of Wild West days. The kids talked about it for days. My daughter Gretchen was excitedly anticipating the event. When we arrived in Jackson Hole the town square was so jammed it was impossible to see anything. Gretchen was heart-broken. Then Mother remembered the camper. Why didn't we use the roof? We climbed the ladder to our "patio," and it was like having front-row seats. The lifelike shoot-'em-up made more of an impression on Gretchen than the Grand Tetons had.

It was a most successful and enjoyable vacation. Our short weekend trips around home had taught us how to live in the camper, but on this long journey we learned that we had a certain independence, going by camper, that no other mode of travel offered. We were self-contained and could take any kind of weather without any discomfort. On the way home we ran into a small tornado. Of course we weren't in the center of it, but we took some rather heavy weather. The gale-force winds struck while we were at a field trial in Wisconsin. In minutes the place was a shambles. Some of the families that had set up tents for the weekend lost everything. We were as snug as a bug.

For many ensuing summers we planned different trips. Our camper never failed us, and we got back into some rather rugged country. We made one addition to our unit for a trip into Canada's bush country. We put in civilian band radio because we were going into territory where help would be difficult to find if we had no means to call for it. We never did need it for an emergency, but we found another use for it. One evening, while listening to some of the talk on the radio, I got an idea. I joined into the radio conversation. My radio friends were in separate towns about thirty miles from us. I asked if they would do me a favor and call by phone collect to our families in the United States, give them the message that we were O.K., and ask what news they had for us. They said they would be glad to do it and they'd call us back in one hour to tell us if they had been successful. The trick worked fine, and we used it often. It also gave us a sense of security, knowing we could summon help if needed.

We put over 100,000 miles on that camper and except for the original problems of springs, battery, and tires we never had any trouble. If I knew then what I know now I might not have sold it. I could have put a new chassis and cab under her and she'd have been as good as new. But that's not what happened. In the eight years we had our camper a lot had taken place in the industry.

Our first little camper was tent-living with a shelter. If the weather didn't permit using the tents, it was too small to make us comfortable for any period of time. Facilities for housekeeping were very crude . . . one step better than tent camping. The camper on the truck body was a big advance in the art of living on wheels. It provided enough space to make daily living easy. Of course, the appliances in the truck camper were still primitive. Water was drawn from the storage tank with a galley pump—nothing really wrong with that; it was a fool-proof system. We made our hot water on the stove. We had a portable toilet that worked fine. To set up the shower we made was a chore, but we managed. There was only one sink, so it doubled for bathroom and kitchen use. Sleeping was of the double-bed variety, and you had to enjoy sleeping with your partner. The heater kept us warm enough, but sometimes an extra pair of socks helped. At times it got pretty hot in the summer but no worse than any other non-air-conditioned house. The one hanging closet was small for a whole family, but I don't remember any fights over that. When we entertained in the camper some people had to stand or sit on the floor, but we always had a good time. The cab got rather hot when we drove in the heat of a summer day, but we opened the windows and got the breeze, plus some dirt. It all added up to pretty good living.

A POSH ADDRESS ON WHEELS

Each year, as our unit got older, new ones with added comforts came out. The basic concept of the camper, a trailer built on a pick-up truck, was only an interim plan. Many years earlier, when I met the builder of my camper, he had told me of his dream. It was someday to build a house on wheels from the tires up. He described then what we know now as the motor home. The capital investment was the thing that held him back, but I knew even then that it was going to happen some day.

It did. Motor homes were now a reality. Soon we would have to make a big decision. Should we spend the money for a major motor overhaul for the camper? The decision was made for us when we stepped into one of the new motor homes. These units were like a Fifth Avenue apartment on wheels—sleeping quarters, lounge area, complete bathroom, thermostatically controlled forced-air heater, air-conditioning when mobile or stationary, a power plant generating enough electricity to run literally a complete house with all its appliances, tap water with the same pressure as at home.

There is a lot of luxury living built into these units, and that means a lot of very complex mechanical things to tend to. In our first little VW camper, the only thing mechanical, except for the engine, was the button on the stove. Today's units have thermostats, pumps, electric gauges, rheostats, pressure gauges, converters, chargers, fans, circuit breakers, valves, air filters, evaporators . . . along with shag rugs.

When my neighbor Frank saw us drive up to our house in a new motor home, he leaned on his rake and shook his head. There was no wine to christen this unit. The neighbors were so awed by the gadgets that they forgot about a celebration.

Again we spent a spring building in the little extras for our own personal comforts, and then we were off doing our thing. In the meantime, our thing had changed. I had become interested in soaring and had bought a competition sailplane, and we were off each weekend to one glider-port or another. We were now quite a sight going down the road; behind our motor home we pulled a thirty-foot trailer that held the disassembled sailplane.

We lived right on the airports in the luxury of a modern motel but without the inconveniences. The new motor home even had aircraft radio, transmitter and receiver, built into it.

We took our new luxury home to a regional soaring competition in the mountains of Vermont. This is very exciting country, and I looked down on every inch of that ski country from the Massachusetts border to the Canadian line. Olive, acting as ground crew, followed every inch of the way under me in the motor home. We kept in radio contact. On those occasions when I couldn't make the flight back to the airfield, I'd be forced to land in a farmer's field. This proved to be quite a happening for the farmer and his family. Unfortunately for me, all the farmers' daughters I met were under ten years old. Even if I'd met a beautiful farmer's daughter what could I have done? My good wife would roll up into the field in a few minutes to retrieve me and the plane.

I am convinced that I would not have become as active in this sport as I did without the motor home. To enter this type of competition I'd have had to fly almost every weekend in the year to gain the experience and the hours of practice that it took. The price of meals and motels would have prevented my doing it.

Vacations took a new twist. We'd spend ten days flying a national event and then be off for a rest in our motor home. It lacked none of the comforts. I relished my morning shower and enjoyed the evening drink in the lounge. We had stereo radio and tape that gave us better quality music than we had at home. People gravitated to our house on wheels, and I liked that. On days when the weather was bad, "hangar flying" took place in our unit. There was no better place to watch the start of a contest day than from our "roof garden."

With the motor home, I got into all sorts of new activities. What a vantage point for watching the take-offs! I flew 200 miles that day. Dinner was late.

As I write this I have a letter on my desk that will be posted in the morning. It's addressed to the maker of one of the major appliances in my motor home. It's a letter making the final arrangements to have the third refrigerator put into my unit. Two have now failed. The manufacturers are standing behind their product. This exchange won't cost me a penny, but it sure has caused a lot of inconvenience. I've written this book so you will know some of the things that the salesman won't tell you, because in most cases he doesn't know. This is such a fast-growing industry that it's moving more rapidly than its own technology. Everyone is going at high gear and they are cutting corners to meet competitive pricing. We'll tell you how to handle this problem of quality control.

As you read you'll see that I speak firmly and to the point, but remember that I still live every weekend in our motor home. Let me give an example. We were at a regional soaring championship in the western part of Virginia. I'd had a very difficult flight that day. The mountains were treacherous. The weather was marginal, and my flight consisted of a series of saves at tree-top level that had me as tight as a drum. After many hours I finally got around the 160-mile course and got back to my home field. I was wrung out. It was hot, and I was exhausted. It was one of those days when you ask yourself, "Why did I ever take up this sport? Golf would be simpler." Then you remember that it was only the day before that you sat at 8000 feet and had a sensational flight. But for this day, forget it! I was greeted on landing with the news that the refrigerator wasn't working and we'd lose our food if something wasn't done about it . . . fast.

It was the second time this had happened. So you can see why we'll talk about this sort of thing.

We'll also tell you how to live on wheels and learn to enjoy it in spite of some of the frustrations. You are going to have to know what to look for when you buy your unit, and how to choose the best one for your needs. Living on wheels is going to be new for many people. There are a lot of tricks to make it easy, and we'll cover what our years have taught us.

Each year newsstands carry a recreation-vehicle catalog in magazine format that will tell what the different manufacturers are making. These publications are by no means complete. There are so many recreation vehicles that these catalogs can cover only one model of each of the major manufacturers. This book is not intended to be such a catalog.

There are a number of trailer and motor-home magazines on your newsstand. Because of the nature of magazines and their dependence on the advertiser for their revenue they can't tell all sides of a story without biting the hand that feeds them. We'll tell it here as we have seen it. That's not always complimentary to the manufacturers . . . but it'll help you.

This is a picture from a magazine advertisement. It's the way the industry presents the motor-home life to the public. It's not very realistic. We'll tell you what it will be like, what to look for—and let the chips fall where they may.

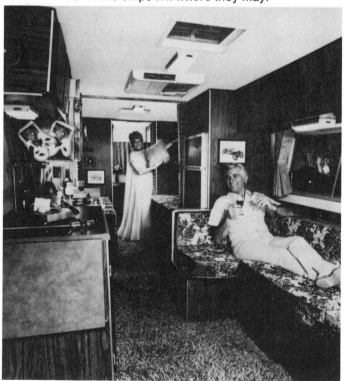

PART II
LIVING ON WHEELS

Living on wheels? It's really nothing new; all through history the go-getters have been doing it. It's been going on ever since the wheel was invented. The expansion and development of our own country came about by a lot of folks putting their households on wheels and moving West. The only thing that stopped them was the Pacific. You're getting into the act when the state of the art is rather sophis-ticated.

Once you have read this book and are daydreaming about sitting in your trailer, camper, or motor home with the evening to kill after you've washed the dishes in hot water, cleaned the stainless-steel sink, tidied up the stove and oven, put the leftovers back in the refrigerator, vacuumed the outdoor-indoor carpet, put a favorite tape on the hi fi, folded away the table and converted the area to a lounge, turned up the thermostat or turned on the air conditioner, switched on the reading lamp . . . pick up a copy of *The Prairie Traveler* by Captain Randolph B. Marcy and see what a similar book written in 1859 suggested. I recommend this reading to convince you that you will have a relatively elegant way of life ahead, living on wheels.

Captain Marcy brings up subjects that I'm not going to discuss. For example, he debates whether to use oxen or mule power; I'll stick to horsepower. He out and out tells you who in Concord, New Hampshire, makes the best wagon. I don't think it proper for an author to push the product of any one company. I only find one fault with his book: he spent a lot of time describing how to ford streams and rivers. I suggest it's much cheaper in the long run just to pay the tolls and use the super-highway bridges.

Many years ago when I became interested in fly fishing, I read as much as possible on the subject before going out to spend my hard-earned money on gear. Becoming confused, I sought the advice of a good friend, America's leading fly fisherman, Lee Wulff. He suggested the finest rod made, then told me it didn't make much difference what rod he suggested, because I'd only do what everybody else did. He was right. He told me to buy a hundred-dollar bamboo rod, but I figured a twenty-dollar glass one would do just as well; so that's what I bought. His prediction was correct. Two rods later I bought the hundred-dollar rod and gave the first two away, for a total expenditure of $140. The moral of the story is to buy the best you can afford at the start.

I have no ax to grind. I sell nothing. The motor home is a way of life with me. On the basis of thirteen years' experience, the purpose of this book is to help you make the decisions you will be faced with, solve as many as possible of the problems that will inevitably arise, and generally make your living on wheels easier. We won't talk much about pop-up tents, tent trailers, pick-up covers, or any fold-away arrangement that will be a compromise between roughing it and the comforts you have at home. The life-style we'll be talking about should not be confused with camping; this living will be as convenient as living at home.

Let's face it. You have lived in a house from before the time you can remember. When it comes time to obtain one for yourself you have a pretty good idea of how it should be constructed and what it should contain. You should also have an idea of how much you can spend.

But too many Americans get trapped: they don't really know what they should spend for a house. Their home becomes their life, not their base for living. After the monthly bills are paid, they have little left over to get out and do things.

The life-style today for many families is full of pressures and tensions. We have it in our jobs. We can't avoid it even in suburbia. We are living in an age when all of the geographic and many of the personal frontiers have been explored, documented, and put on television. Is there any real adventure any more? How does one break out and find a change of pace, a change of scene, and become a doer? The answer for many families is to pick up and go in a motor home or trailer.

Our clothing is a good example of our new-found freedom. When your wife plays tennis, she wears a nice little white tennis dress . . . and that's about it. When her great-grandmother played, one hand held her skirt and the rest of her was held by a corset. Try that on your backhand. The trend in housing is indoor-outdoor living, and a trailer or motor home fits into the new scheme of things.

IS A HOUSE ON WHEELS FOR YOU?

Living on wheels can be more expensive than motel and restaurant living. It's all a numbers game. How many times a year are you going to use your vehicle or go to the trouble of motel living?

33

Motels are expensive; you pay for all the modern decor and swimming pools even if you rarely use them, and some of us can remember eating for a whole week for the price of a good dinner on the road today. Cooking in your own motor home is cheaper, faster, and you'd better agree with me when I say it's better. But even if you have a large family, so that the costs of these services add up fast, it will be cheaper going the motel route if you're only using the vehicle for the annual family vacation. It's true that day-to-day costs in a recreation vehicle are less than the motel route, but to buy an RV takes a big chunk of cash which could buy a lot of nights at a motel or trips abroad. I'm not crazy about motel travel. I dislike the lugging, unpacking, and arranging, all of which I can do without after ten hours behind the wheel. But you can't use that as an excuse to spend $10,000; it's just another frustration and our lives are full of them.

The only logical way of considering a home on wheels is to think of it as your second home. You wouldn't consider it good economics to buy a cottage on the beach if you were only going to use it for the few weeks of yearly vacation. If you are buying a second house you've got to consider more than the fact that you can live in it without paying any more for food and utilities than at home. Buying a beach house is an investment that will tie up a big chunk of capital. It's the same with a motor home or a luxury trailer—only more so, because they won't increase in value like a home, but will depreciate.

Escape seems to be more and more on the minds of the American public. The prairie traveler made his trip for economic reasons; ours are more apt to be psychological and sociological. A second house, a boat, or a motor home could easily be the escape route.

Along with our desire to escape, we Americans have another characteristic—we buy impulsively. I've known some folks who became fascinated with a little cottage in the mountains. They bought it and spent all kinds of time and money making it into their dream house. What they didn't realize was that the work, the planning, the sense of creating and building was their real pleasure. Two years later they became bored by the isolation and soon felt trapped by their investment of money and sweat. I've also known families who became infatuated by the motor home concept but soon became disillusioned for a reason they failed to anticipate. There is something very appealing about a compact, modern, luxurious RV. One family I knew became swept up in the excitement of a local RV show. They put their money up and spent a lot of time outfitting their vehicle. They threw a gala farewell party in it before they left for a month's trip to the Coast. A year later they sold it. After talking to them, I figured out what happened. Wherever they went they had the feeling of not belonging. I was surprised that they fell for the RV concept in the first place. They were more the country club or beach club type. Some people need the security of a social structure around their home base and are lost without it. It takes a certain amount of adventuresomeness for this way of life. It won't be a roughing-it adventure, with the luxury you're going to have, but the spirit of adventure has to be there. I don't mean to turn this into a sociological treatise, but you are going to have to know yourself well before you make the investment of a second house, whether it be on a foundation or on wheels.

There is no way advising exactly in your decision whether or not to buy a motor home, because each person or family has a different set of circumstances. Age has a lot to do with the decision. The average age for those buying the more expensive motor home is the early fifties. The reasons for this seem obvious. First, young people are still building families and paying for the prime house. This takes money. But there is a new trend in this country in family structure. The idea of building a family homestead in the sense of a house that will be occupied by several generations no longer exists. Distances have been shortened by modern modes of transportation. It's the same for both country and city people. As a result, children often no longer stay in the community in which they were raised. Building a home and expecting your children to live in it is a thing of the past. The first world war brought people to the cities; the second war made them world travelers.

The first generation of parents who had their families dispersed became lost souls. The high points of their year were their occasional trips to visit the kids. The second generation of such parents realized the old homestead was too big, and by the millions they have been moving to apartments, buying motor homes and trailers, and taking full advantage of their freedom and leisure time.

But the advantages of living on wheels have also been recognized by countless younger families. I was nowhere near retirement age when we started living our weekends on wheels, and I'm nowhere near it now. What happened in our case, and in the case of many motor-home owners I have interviewed, was that we all recognized that the older generation had stumbled onto something pretty good and we saw no reason to wait until retirement to join them.

We have come to know many retired couples who have settled completely on the vagabond life and follow the seasons around the country. Living on wheels has become a younger and younger way of life.

A NEW LIFE-STYLE

It makes no difference what vehicle you settle on, whether it be trailer, camper, mini-motor home, or a motor home thirty feet long, *living on wheels will change your life-style.* In my own case, I couldn't settle and live in a second home because I wasn't sure which area of the country would keep me satisfied. I knew I'd be happy if I could take a little of all of them, a ski lodge and a place on the beach. Now with an RV I have them both. Many years ago, before I had my first RV, I learned a lesson when I became an avid fly fisherman. I was casting one day with a famous trout fisherman, Wes Jordan. He was the foremost rod maker and designer in the country and would fish at the drop of a hat, if it had flies on its band. I told him of my desire to own a fishing shack on the edge of just such a stream as the one we were fishing that day.

He reeled in his line, stepped out of the stream, took out his pipe, sat on a rock, and took his merry time to say, "That's a stupid idea."

My facial response was no surprise to him.

36

"I've seen so many guys try it," he said, "but it doesn't work. O.K., you buy a place. Then you start putting it into shape. Right there you've lost a full season or two of fishing. Then you get it so nice that people start dropping in . . . might even have to add a small wing. The driveway will need repair; so will the roof. Then at last, the year you have everything under control, there's a drought and the fishing in the area is ruined. Make up your mind! Do you want to be a property owner or do you want to fish?"

He picked up his rod, stepped back into his pool, and started a fine long false cast. A year later I bought my first RV and fished all the good streams everywhere. Old Mr. Jordan had taught me a good lesson.

There was another facet to Jordan's advice. When I did start this weekend living on wheels, it soon became evident that my little VW camper was to become more than a mobile fishing shack. When the fishing season ended, as it does each fall, I wasn't about to put the traveling house up for the winter. I found new sports and interests to take me around the four seasons. My gasoline bills went up, but so did my enjoyment. Life was full of new places, new friends, new activities, and some new expenses—I had to pay the kid down the street to keep my lawn cut and the professional painter had to be called in every so often. After all, I did have an obligation to my house investment. But the family had more fun being off going and doing, and I liked the idea better than staying home being a gardener, farmer, and handyman. They were subjects I never studied in college, anyway.

AN INDUSTRY IS BORN

When I drove my latest motor home up to the house to show it off proudly to the family, our daughter took one look at it and gave it its name—"The Breadbox." That was pretty good: it was white, it was square shaped, and it did look like a breadbox. At dinner that evening I complimented her on the imaginative name, then went into a rather long discussion about industrial design. I pointed out that this breadbox shape was functional, dictated by a new method of bonded foam wall construction and the interior needs of the unit.

I felt rather intelligent expounding this theory of design, but I could see by the expression on Gretchen's face that we were on different wave lengths. I stopped my showing off and asked her what was wrong. "Daddy, I didn't name it 'The Breadbox' because it looks like one; I named it that because all your dough is tied up in it!" I picked up my fork and went to work on my plate. How right Gretchen was! I did have a lot of my dough in it.

Later that evening, when Olive and I were sitting in the elegant lounge of the new breadbox, we couldn't help but compare it to the little VW we had bought more than twelve years earlier. We would never have believed back in those days that the industry could have possibly come up with such improvements and added comforts. This was not a conversion, an adaptation—it was a whole new concept. What had been created was a new way of life on wheels. A whole industry had not only been born, in a very few years it had become adult.

AN INDUSTRY IS BORN

Manufacturers start with a chassis and build the house on the wheels.

Above: The chassis is modified and strengthened to take floor and walls of bonded foam construction. In this, the most popular type of construction, a sandwich is made of Styrofoam bonded between an aluminum exterior and plywood interior. *Right:* Bonded floor being made. *Bottom:* Floor is placed on chassis. Dashboard is already in place.

In the top picture the water and electrical systems and propane gas tanks are installed. As the vehicle moves down the assembly line (*lower picture*) the cabinets and appliances are added. The cabinets are built in the woodworking shop and completed after being put in place.

40

The motor home starts to take shape as the walls go on. Windows will be installed, the whole unit weather-sealed. Each assembly line handles a different model. The capacity of the Winnebago factory is astonishing. In RVs from this plant alone hundreds and hundreds of new families are on the road each week seeking a new life-style.

A NAME . . . AND SOME DEFINITIONS

Today there are recreation vehicles priced within the reach of millions of American families. They range all the way from tent trailers that pop up within seconds to make sleeping, eating, and living quarters and cost less than a thousand dollars, to thirty-foot trailers and full bus-length custom motor homes, some of which carry a price tag of more than fifty thousand.

This new industry is so young that the names of the types of vehicles haven't even been sorted out. Some manufacturers even compound the confusion by using different terms for the same vehicle. No wonder the prospective buyer has difficulty. Although we'll be discussing mainly the larger self-contained units in this book, it seems a good idea to get all the definitions set straight.

The place to begin is with that word "self-contained." The easiest way of understanding what we mean by that is simply to consider what you have in your family house. Surely your home is self-contained: all the facilities for living are there, ready to be used whenever they are needed. It's almost the same on wheels, but there are degrees of being self-contained. The most complete recreation vehicle will require no outside services. You'll have your own water, heat, kitchenette, refrigeration, bed, toilet and sewer system, bathing and storage spaces. You'll generate your own electricity for whatever number of home appliances you wish to carry for your convenience. You'll enjoy air-conditioning. You name it, and it's now possible to have it along. Some of the top-priced, custom-made units have both dish and clothes washers. In a completely self-contained RV you carry along all the same facilities you have at home.

The most inexpensive way to go on wheels is with the . . .

These are trailers with folding shelters that range from simple tents to elaborate folding walls which form expanding sections to provide a lot of living space and good protection from summer storms. They carry water, ice box, food compartments, cooking facilities, and ample sleeping arrangements that are off the ground. They take only a few minutes to rig and de-rig.

. . . camping trailer. It goes up in only a few minutes. It has a built-in sink, stove and even refrigerator and heater. It'll sleep the whole family and the most complete units cost only a few thousand dollars.

There is a trailer in a size for every pocketbook, from ten footers . . .

TRAVEL TRAILERS

Trailers are non-powered living coaches or houses on wheels designed to be towed. They have rigid tops and walls and range in length from ten to thirty feet and up to eight feet wide. There are a lot of new developments in trailers. The fifth-wheel concept comes

. . . to thirty, and no matter what size they are elegant living.

from the hook-up principle used in semi-trucks. These units are towed by a pick-up truck. This makes pulling a trailer very safe since the weight is located between the axles rather than behind them. These fifth wheelers give a lot of living space for relatively low cost.

"Fifth wheel" design is shown at left. The pick-up truck is the "fifth wheel." The bedroom is up forward and windows surround the large social area at rear. On the right is a fun design. The caboose is fitted out with train lanterns and Victorian decor like the old-time steam cars. It's even painted bright red. The bottom picture shows just how elegant life can be on the interstate highways from coast to coast.

TRUCK CAMPERS

There are basically two kinds of campers: the slide-in unit and the chassis mount. The advantage of the slide-in is that the truck can be used for other work. Campers usually have a cab-over, a section that contains a bed and extends over the truck cab. They are measured, however, from the rear of the truck cab to the rear of the box, and range from eight to twelve feet in length. They do not provide the best use of space, but you get a lot for your dollar value. The chassis-mounted rigs will slowly be replaced by the mini-motor home.

The pick-up camper is the first step toward the motor home. It is like a trailer carried on a truck bed. These units cost from $2000 to $4000 plus the truck's cost. They can sleep as many as eight with at-home comfort.

46

Fold-down jacks make it an easy job to take the house off the truck. The truck can now be used for work during the week, a motel on weekends.

Chassis-mount pick-ups, the truck bed removed, give more living space.

MINI-MOTOR HOME

The mini is the one that's called by many names: some call it a slash van and some give it the full title of motor home. It's a van-type truck with the body replaced aft of the doors. Mini-motor homes come in models from seventeen to twenty feet in length and offer a good use of space. They are priced in the $8,000 range and provide a lot of self-containment. The major difference between the campers and the mini is that the mini has walk-through access between the driving and living areas—an important feature when traveling.

The mini is a real improvement on chassis-mount units. With all its conveniences, it should get the full title of motor home.

Van campers are also called van conversions. They are stock vans that have been fitted with the basic appliances and sleeping accommodations. Some are Spartan affairs, while others are ingenious in their use of space. Many feature roof cutouts and various types of mechanisms for raising the ceiling and providing standup headroom. There is going to be more and more development in van campers because they can truly be used as a second family car. Living in most such units is really togetherness, but for the sports-minded family on the go they offer a lot. For about $11,000, the top of the van camper lines, you can have small versions of the same appliances you have in a truck camper . . . even a shower.

Van campers are of two types, those that are simple conversions and those that are a major redesign of the factory production models. It's' fun for me to see how they have improved the VW from the first one that we had (above). Below is a standard Dodge made into a weekend home. It is tight living but can be fun.

49

This is luxury. The basic unit has been rebuilt and lengthened, insulated and given the living comforts of a motor home. It will sleep four with comfort, is air conditioned and heated, and has a full bathroom with shower and plenty of storage space. It's small enough to use as a second car. We are going to see more of these around.

The motor homes are the glamour rigs. They are built from the ground up using a standard truck chassis. Although they are usually twenty to twenty-eight feet long, many manufacturers are coming in with small units to try to capture the market from the van conversions. The smaller eighteen-footers are competitive in price with the van conversions. The motor home is self-propelled and is the last word in self-containment with all the options it can accommodate.

Apollo

Chinook

Sightseer

Superior

Avco

Starcraft

Unlimited luxury is available for the price. This converted bus by Wake-
field is a plush apartment on wheels. The cost starts at around $50,000
and can go as high as $150,000. The makers will build into it any feature
you wish. It's a push-buttom dream: beds move into position by electric
motors and there is a complete laundry aboard.

WHAT WE'LL BE TALKING ABOUT

To explain just how one should live on wheels, we will talk most
about the motor home since it offers the most convenience and ease
in operation. It should be remembered at the same time that the
travel trailer can be just as self-contained as a motor home. Many
of the problems we will discuss apply to all the RVs.

The speed with which this American RV industry has grown is
truly amazing. For example, in 1965 there were under 5000 motor
homes built. In 1972, over 60,000 motor homes were put on the
road. The industry is talking about 1,000,000 being on the highways by 1980. In some ways the industry has grown too fast. This
leads to problems. There would be no need for this book if I were

just going to repeat in it everything put out by the manufacturers in their slick, four-color brochures. In some areas I'm afraid the manufacturers and designers have made mistakes on their drawing boards. It's a mushrooming business and they have to battle costs. But that shouldn't be your worry when you're off on holiday in 100-degree weather and the refrigeration doesn't work.

After all, as my daughter said, Daddy's dough is in it. If you get the feeling that I am against the industry, you will be getting the wrong impression. But I strongly feel that the RV designers, as well as owners, can learn something by reading this book. I don't set myself up as Ralph Nader, but I would like to persuade the manufacturers of motor homes to take their families out on the road in their products. Besides the fun they'll have trying to fix the refrigerator, they'll find some other things right under their noses that should be changed. More testing, under everyday, hot-and-cold, rain-or-shine conditions is desperately needed . . . and we'll talk about it.

WHICH ONE . . . TRAILER, CAMPER, MINI- OR MAXI-MOTOR HOME?

If we could all agree; if all our needs were the same; if we all had the same income, same size family, same hobbies—we wouldn't need four major automobile manufacturers. On my commuter train I've seen arguments over who had the best car almost come to blows. Now how am I going to tell you how to pick a luxury RV for your living pleasure?

There is a vehicle for almost every family who can afford a second car. The problem is that the choice is extremely varied and the history of the development of this industry will demonstrate some of the answers that others before you have found.

It all began with the trailer. At first simple and crude, it evolved over the years into an extremely luxurious self-contained unit. The market was large enough so that manufacturers saw a big thing coming and developed modern appliances on a miniature scale that would have dazzled the housewife of only a few years ago.

Hooking this house on wheels to the family car seemed at first to be a real convenience, and for some it still is. Then someone had the bright idea to make it piggy-back. The pick-up truck was used for this. This fitted into the automotive manufacturers' scheme of things. They were interested in this market. The lowly pick-up became a rather luxurious means of transportation. It really wasn't like a truck any more. It was designed so that the wife could drive it and be just as comfortable as she was in the family car. Interiors were spruced up with color, air-conditioning, and the same gadgets found in a car. In certain areas of the country this was seen by the manufacturers as the family's second car. Fitting a trailer on top of a pick-up truck opened up a whole new market.

The first camper was built to slide into the truck bed. This put limitations on its size. All sorts of ingenious devices were tried, even an overhang that rode on its own wheels. One solution to the problem was to remove the bed and build the "trailer" directly onto the chasis. This defeated the original idea of using the pick-up truck as double duty—a family car and work horse during the week and the family motel on the weekend. But the idea took. Big units were built and the interiors were as fine as in the best trailers.

The chassis-mount eliminating the pick-up bed seemed to be logical, but basically the design is wrong. The separate cab area makes inefficient use of space in a vehicle where every inch counts. The natural evolution was a design that started from the wheels up—the motor home, the trailer its Momma and the pick-up camper its Pa. It's got the best features of both. It's interesting to note that the offspring started off bigger than its parents. The first trailers and campers were both small. The motor home is a big baby. The motor-home industry started with big, lavish units and is only now working down to smaller sizes. Seventeen- and eighteen-foot units are now competitive in price with campers. Of course, some twenty-eight-footers are competitive in price with Morgan's yacht.

The development of the small motor home and the mini-motor home, with most of the advantages of the bigger models, has put these RV units into the price range of many more families.

TRAILER OR MOTOR HOME?

The real advantage of a trailer is that you can park it on a property and leave it hooked up to utilities all year round. If you wish, you can use it only on weekends. In that way, it's a second home. You also have the advantage of being able to take it on a vacation trip. A trailer truly serves as a weekend house and as your motel. The financial investment involved is relatively small.

For the money, a trailer offers a lot of convenient living. It's not as mobile as the self-propelled units, but if traveling and just going places to stay for a while is what you wish to do, a trailer can serve you well. The larger units are slow on the road, but even this can be offset by the fact that once you do arrive, you're going to have a comfortable way of living.

Another advantage of the trailer is that when you park it you have your home site staked out and the car becomes your local transportation. Campers and motor homes have to stake their claims by leaving a tent or some chairs at the site when they go to town. There are other ways to solve that problem. One is the motor bike. It's easy to lift it off the bumper rack and go off to town to do the shopping . . . except if it's raining or if the whole family wants to go. The other answer to that problem is to tow a Jeep or other small car behind. We've met a number of retired couples who live all year in their motor homes. They tow the family car.

If you tow a small car, side trips are no problem. Keep the motor home on the campsite.

Carry extra wheels with you. The ecology-minded use the noiseless bicycle. Racks are commercially available. This kind of travel will add to your fun on wheels.

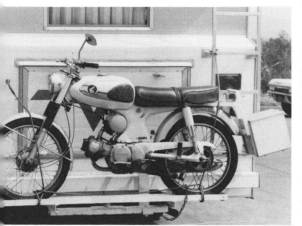

If you are involved in a sport which requires towing something else, of course you can't do it with a trailer. This is an advantage of the self-propelled RVs. You can tow even a thirty-foot sailplane on the tow hitch, and off you go to do your thing anywhere. Most states have a fifty-five-foot limit. Take note of the different things towed behind all kinds of vehicles on the roads these days. People are taking equipment for every conceivable sport along with them: racing cars, horses, snowmobiles, sailplanes, sail boats, fishing boats, duck boats, and dog carriers for field trials, to name just a few.

Discussing the question of whether to choose a motor home or trailer, the president of the country's largest RV company com-

Guess what it is. A sailplane in its trailer! RV living gets you out doing things.

mented: "Money could be the most important factor in determining which way to go. A motor home represents a bigger cash outlay. If money is not the issue, the buyer has to decide how he is going to use the unit. If he is going to go someplace and sit a spell, a trailer will suit him fine. If he is going to be on the go, participate in sports, do a lot of moving about, a motor home is the answer. There is a lot of convenience to traveling right in your own house."

RENT FIRST? . . . THEN BUY?

If you want to have a vacation in a trailer or self-contained motor home as a one-time experience, of course you'll rent a unit. Although renting is rather costly, nevertheless, if you are serious about buying an RV, and have no previous experience of living in confined mobile quarters, renting first should be considered. If you have been doing a lot of tent-camping or living on a boat in a confined space, you have a good background for RV living, or if you and the family have been dreaming about owning a self-contained recreational vehicle and have been doing your homework for a long time, the cost of the rental could be a waste of money. On the other hand, if Aunt Nellie has just left you a chunk of cash and you and your wife wonder whether this RV life would suit you, rent first. You've got to know a lot about yourself, the family, the RV industry and what it offers. Is your wife going to like living in a small house? Will cooking in cramped quarters send her up the wall? Do you like to tinker and take care of gadgets? If you aren't sure how your family is going to respond to living on wheels . . . rent first.

SOME TIPS FOR THE NEW WAY

Before either renting or buying, it will be helpful to know some of the special tricks you'll have to learn.

Although we'll discuss storing things in more detail later, it should be said here that all adults should pack their own things. We start doing this in the house. First, make a list and don't forget nights and mornings can be cold in the summertime. We put all items into a clothes hamper and carry it out to the motor home. Each person has assigned cabinet space and puts his own things away so he'll know where they are. With all we seem to cram in, it's not much fun to discover later, on the road, that we forgot the crystal champagne glasses and silver ice bucket.

To make the job easier for mother, every adult takes care of his own clothes. Packing is a science . . . that is, if you want to find the things you know you have brought along.

We carry mainly wash-and-wear clothes for the particular season of the year, but we make sure that we have clothing for the most extreme fluctuations for that season.

RV living is supposed to be a form of escape, getting away from it all. Nothing will send the wife up the wall faster than having to do all the work. If you're just putting her to work on wheels, it isn't much fun. People, even members of the same family, are not used to living so close together. The unit has to be always kept neat. One slob in the group can really set everyone on edge. Clothes must be put away, out of sight, back in their place—in fact, that goes for everything. Any mess has to be cleaned up right away. Everyone has to do his part. You'll find that it makes for some pretty good living.

All meals should be as simple as possible; while traveling we use salads, sandwiches, or canned stews. Paper plates and cups help a lot.

Water conservation is something all aboard have to learn.

Showers are of the navy variety: first a wet-down, then a soap-down, then a rinse. After a shower the curtain should be shaken to get the water off it. Each adult should sponge the floor after his shower is over. It's a small space, but you'll get used to the system. Underclothes and towels stay in the stall with you. They won't get wet if they're stored on the hook and racks with the shower curtain closed all around. We use a bathmat outside the shower. I honestly enjoy my morning shower more in the motor home than at home. It's hard to say why, just a feeling about it.

There is one problem. Often in the summer we do not leave the hot-water heater on all night; this conserves bottled gas. We keep the pilot lit but we've got to run outside to turn the thermostat up. Why the makers haven't solved this problem yet with an inside hot-water control is beyond me. They'll finally come to their senses. In the meantime, I have to run out in my pajamas to flick the knob up! The point of all this is that I wear very plain, dark-colored pajamas. That way, when I go outside, I don't look as though I were running around in my pj's. I wonder what Captain Marcy would say about that.

Dish washing should be kept to a minimum to conserve both Mom and the water. Some day they'll invent a small dishwasher that will use recycled water and propane to bring the water to the boiling point for sterilization. Until it comes, dishes will have to be done by hand. A double sink is good for this purpose. In some units such a sink is optional, along with the floor plan. For our latest unit we ordered a fold-down tabletop to extend the kitchen work space. If it's not optional in the unit you select, it's easy enough to make one yourself.

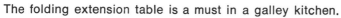
The folding extension table is a must in a galley kitchen.

Dishes are washed in one of the sinks in very little soapy water. They are rinsed in the second sink with a tea kettle of boiling water. Rinse by pouring very little water into glasses and bowls, swishing it around, and then pouring it onto the next item. This proves to be a very efficient way of doing it.

Once a day, after breakfast, we take five minutes and clean the unit. We carry a child's broom, which takes up very little space, for just that purpose. There are very small vacuum cleaners that can be had for little money. The point is that anything you can do to make the household chores as easy and as fast as possible is going to make Mom happier. Some women just won't buy this recreation vehicle way of life. They feel that when vacation time comes they want someone else to be doing the work. If that woman can put up with light housework, her two- or three-week vacation can be expanded to every weekend with an RV. Some women don't mind the work; they enjoy the change of scenery. Renting a vehicle is going to give you a real test of your attitudes about this kind of living.

Renting a unit will also soon show whether or not the man of the wheeled household is going to blow his spare. Some men have a hard time zipping their own jackets, and for them, RV living may be just too much. We've seen it happen. There is a lot to see to, but it's not difficult. If a fellow is the kind that likes to tinker he'll do just fine. Just like a house, no recreation vehicle comes through from the builder with all the gadgets and do-dads; if a fellow isn't handy, or doesn't want to be, he may not like to live on wheels. This is the time to find out. This is also the time to find out whether he can handle a trailer on the back of a car. Trailers make some people nervous wrecks. The same thing could apply to some folks' trying to push around a big motor home. If you have any doubts, try it out. You'll most likely find it's no big problem . . . but at least you'll know.

We know of one family who finally decided that their kids were too young for this kind of living. What they were really saying was that the kids would drive the wife crazy all day in a one-room house. It's good to find out things like this first, before the money goes down. Kids, even older ones, can get pretty rambunctious being cooped up. We found on our first trip across the country that although Mom and Dad preferred to stop and camp alone at the side of a stream, the kids found it tiresome. The problem was solved by stopping in public camp sites every so often when the kids got restless. Even we enjoyed the social exchange.

Before a dealer sends you off in a unit, he'll go over all the appliances and things you should know to make the trip successful. Sometimes these briefings are not good enough. Make sure you also have the operating manuals and instructions for every appliance. Buy a cassette tape recorder, one of the inexpensive ones, and as the dealer goes around the unit telling you how to run this and that gadget, tape his remarks. It's going to be difficult remembering all he has to say; you'll remember better what you saw him do when you hear it on play-back. Some of the written instructions are not too clear, and the dealer will have some extra little tips.

The whole point is that if you don't expect too much too soon, you're going to be pleasantly surprised. That's all you should be after.

WATCH OUT

Every year the recreation-vehicle industry has a national show to display its wares, but it's not for the public. The purpose of the show is to get dealers to buy the vehicles to sell to you, the buying public. The show is huge; the number of vehicles on display boggles the mind. The fact emerges that the state of the art is such that there are many, many good units available, but none is the ultimate answer.

It is still possible that the ideal unit will be manufactured. It could be designed right from that show by taking individual good features from all the RVs and putting them into one. For example, I saw a unit with an ingenious method of handling dirty laundry. It featured a nine-inch-wide trap door with a chute under it. Snapped to the chute was a laundry bag that hung in a compartment below. It was accessible by an outside door. This manufacturer was using his head. To my knowledge, this was the only unit that had provision for soiled clothes. Next to it was a unit that had no closet for hanging clothes. Possibly it was designed for nudists.

Watch out for impractical decor. The interiors are being designed to attract women who have spent little or no time living on the road. You can see the unskilled hand of the interior designer. He is trying too hard to make the motor home look like a house; he is trying to entice the woman to try the same thing on wheels. It's not practical. Velvet upholstery will look good in a showroom, but not so good after the kids have been out on the beach. Shag rugs in the bathroom and around the toilet are not practical. Fake stained-glass partitions look fine at home but have no place in a motor home. Partitions without a real purpose should be avoided; they only chop up the space. The open, airy look is a must for a long stay in small quarters.

Watch out, also, for color. There is a new trend, the heavy Spanish look. Woodwork is stained dark to give a rich appearance. It does not work. The units are too gloomy. Once again, it looks fine in the showroom or in the color advertisement, but it's psychologically bad and a lot of women may not recognize this until they have been on the road a few weeks.

Fake heavy hardware is another no-no. It is neither functional nor strong. It has that flashy good look that really can't stand scrutiny. Don't be fooled by quilted vinyl doors meant to look like leather. Much money is spent on this kind of useless veneer. Too much time is being spent by manufacturers on the frills and not enough on really useful detail. For example, many of the cupboards and cabinets have splintery raw wood, very few shelves, and unfinished void space behind elegant doors. Try sometime to stack shirts ten deep in such cabinets. They can be used to only half their capacity because no shelf has been provided. It's wrong to put an exquisite door on such a hole.

The crowning blow was the introduction of chandeliers. The one in the photograph is not unique. I had to study it to believe it. I looked for a way to dismantle it for storage while traveling, but it was permanently installed. Who thought of a swinging glass globe to clomp Mother on one side and the wall on the other? Someone

This kind of decorating is an outrage. It's attractive but dangerous.

has to blow the whistle on this sort of planning. As Captain Marcy would say, "It's not the most useful article for a prairie tour."

I mentioned one unit that had no clothes closet, but I did not mention one velvet-upholstered unit of twenty-seven feet that had a door in the front and one closet in the rear. To hang up a wet coat you'd have to walk through the whole unit. That unit displayed candlesticks on the dining table. A sign boasted that the unit could sleep eight . . . with one closet in the rear? Candlesticks at a table that would seat only three? Nothing like the little woman having to feed them in shifts on vacation! In another unit, what looked to be a bathroom of superior design boasted a full-size molded Fiberglas tub as the selling point. When asked about water capacity, the manufacturer's representative seemed hurt. It was the wrong question. The unit had a thirty-gallon capacity and after a few baths you'd be out of water. Bathtubs are fine, but navy showers are a part of RV living.

Look out for decor like that on the left. It indicates that the guy in the showroom knows little about RV living. The reclining bunk bed is good.

SAFETY . . . IT'S ALL ENGINEERING COMMON SENSE

A recreation vehicle show provides an ideal opportunity to compare the products of the different manufacturers from the standpoint of safety. Use your common sense. Walk around the outside of the various units and see, for example, what protrusions there are that the kids can run into while playing. Do doors have sharp edges? Could windows that swing out catch someone in the arm or head? Have the corners been rounded off and smoothed? Could the drainpipes trip someone?

When you've made your outside inspection, step inside the units. Sit in them and visualize what would happen if you were going down the road and suddenly the vehicle had to come to an abrupt halt. Are there seat belts all around? What would happen at 60 miles per hour if someone were fixing a sandwich or the kids were moving about and the brakes were slammed on. What things would start to fly, or what would *you* hit if you went into orbit? Are the tables and seats really secured to the floor or walls? It's not going to do you much good if you are fastened in a seat belt and a piece of furniture comes flying at you. If *you* do the flying, do the protruding armrests have plenty of padding? Do the tables have rounded corners? Are the edges sharp or beveled? How thick is the table? Hitting a thin edge can cause a lot of damage to a person. Congratulations to one manufacturer who padded the edge of the table.

Are the wall and cabinet corners rounded and/or beveled? Do door handles and drawer pulls protrude? The best handles are recessed or flush mounted. The maker who leaves the pulling type hardware off and uses thumb holes or finger slots is not saving a buck; he's thinking of your safety.

All interior doors and cabinet doors should have spring-loaded locking devices. They should not be able to swing open no matter how hard they are jarred or twisted. Otherwise, hit a rut in the road and the stuff in your cabinets will be all over the floor. Or have an accident and if you collide with a cabinet door that has swung open your vacation may come to an end. Sometimes manufacturers consider eye appeal more important than eye safety.

The safest kind of drawers are those that have to be lifted out of a detent or slot and then slide out on a track. Drawer facings should all be beveled or rounded. Refrigerator doors should be recessed into the wooden cabinet and not have the metal edge protruding into the aisle. Don't ask me why stove manufacturers use protruding knobs for kids to play with or adults to bump into!

Notice, too, whether the curtain rods are secured or just hanging in brackets. There is nothing like a spear flying around the inside of a unit in a bad accident. And are the curtains too close to the stove?

A smooth floor is treacherous in an RV. If the unit has a linoleum floor, is it pebbled or rough surfaced? If it is, the maker was thinking of your safety. You should never wax such a floor or use throw rugs. Wall-to-wall carpeting is safest. Long-pile or shag rugs catch heels and cause falls.

How would you get out of the unit if the door was jammed? Is there an escape hatch, a second door, or a window where the screen won't block your getting out fast?

There is one aspect of safety that we can't tell much about by sitting in the units, and that is the construction of the vehicle. There are certain kinds of accidents on our highways that no one could survive . . . they are as lethal as plane crashes. The big argument in the industry today is whether the bonded foam construction used in walls, ceilings, and floors will stand up to a bad crash. Some engineers say the foam will absorb a tremendous amount of impact. This bonded combination consists of an aluminum exterior and a plywood interior; under pressure these are glued to each side of the foam, which forms a sandwich between them. This makes a very strong wall. It also provides the best of all insulation. But are the joints of the walls with the floor and the roof enough to sustain a roll-over? Makers who construct their vehicles with steel supports and Fiberglas walls swear the foam units will split open like a matchbox in an accident. Their arguments sound very good and I suspect they are right. The foam wall makers counter with tensile strength arguments. This argument is in the process of being settled, but it will take time. The National Highway Traffic Safety Administration, part of the Department of Transportation, sets the standards. At the moment they are only investigating . . . and governments move slowly. A few companies are conducting tests on their own.

This accident shows what shocks the bonded foam walls can absorb. This unit hit a bridge abutment. Watch out—the poorest type of construction uses wooden studs with the exterior and interior materials nailed to the studding and Fiberglas insulation placed in the wall.

This is what can happen. In this case the only person aboard was the driver. He walked away unhurt, saved by seat belts. Although there are few statistics on accidents like this, steps are being taken by the manufacturers to improve the safety of the vehicles. An example of what will come about is shown below. The front and rear ends will most likely have steel cages, and they will be tied together with steel in the side walls.

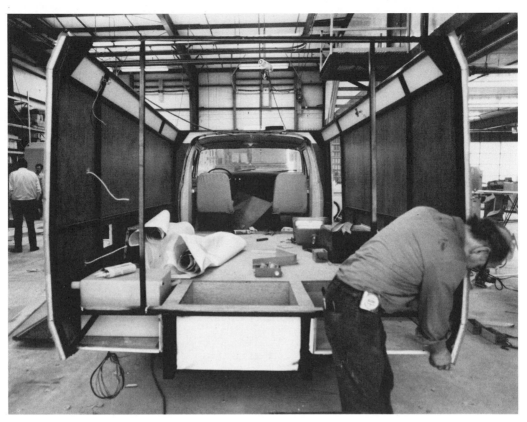

Changes in construction are coming fast. Here steel is being added to the foam core. In certain types of serious accidents, there seems little difference in the people's fate whether steel supports are used or not.

FLOOR PLAN

When you see a recreation vehicle show, it's hard to realize that this industry is still so very young. It certainly offers the public a lot, and in general the products are very well planned. This industry has moved down the road much faster than the boat makers. Tradition seems to have hindered the yachtsman; also the shape and size of a boat hull determine much about the below-deck arrangement. The RV designer is also limited by size and shape, but he has much more flexibility.

The motor-home industry, for example, seems to have gone in

two directions. One is to build a floor plan into the shell, and the other is to build a shell that fits a floor plan. The exterior of the first Winnebagos that appeared on the roads seemed strange and not very aesthetic. Its functionally shaped exterior had its purpose: it gave maximum use of the interior space, and that is what the game is all about. The interior needs dictated the exterior shape. The conventional bus-shaped units are more expensive to construct, but in many of them the designers have learned to use the curves ingeniously. In this business good design is a function of practicality. If aesthetics can also be served, so much the better; and for a price we can do anything.

As we have pointed out, you can see some rather stupid detailing and planning at an RV show where direct comparisons can be made. The public will finally catch on to bad detailing. The difficult part of designing is that there are so many tastes to satisfy that there can be no one authority on the subject. What my wife thinks is a poor floor plan, someone else will buy and like. What, then, do you look for in a floor plan? Once you determine the living requirements you need, the next most important item is spelled out, we think, in one word—openness.

This can best be appreciated by looking at a set of floor plans for two units built to the same exterior measurements but offering different arrangements—one "open" and the other compartmentalized, or "closed in." The two plans shown are offered optionally by one manufacturer. Any plan that has wardrobes and other floor-to-ceiling cabinetry opposite another wall of cabinets, closets, or the bathroom, produces a closed-in corridor. One gets the feeling that he is in the aisle of a Pullman car. It breaks the living space into two segments, front and rear. Not only is ventilating, cooling, or heating such a unit difficult, but the social area is split up. A corridor arrangement may not make for easy living. Doors on one side can't be used while the ones on the other side are in use. People will be constantly trying to pass one another . . . in each other's way.

When I asked an owner of an RV with the corridor plan how he liked it, he agreed that it was a little clumsy but added, "The thing we like about it is that the kids sleep up front and we have the back

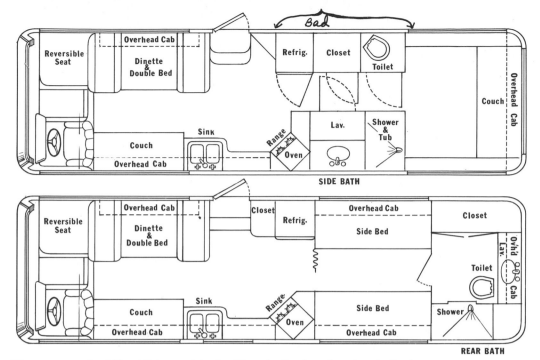

SIDE BATH

REAR BATH

The area marked "bad," in my handwriting, in the top drawing indicates how I feel about this design. The cabinets on both sides of the unit, in the area marked, make a corridor that chops the unit up into front and rear sections. All the doors opening opposite each other make it difficult to move around, especially if more than one person is in that area. Where would you entertain? There seems to be no social center. Heating or air-conditioning such a unit is difficult. The lower plan is good. It's open, with plenty of space to move about, and a social area to seat guests. It's easy to heat and would have good air circulation.

to ourselves." It gave the adults added privacy. To select a floor plan you have to think out all the day and night activities for the family. Designers are just starting to recognize that the social aspects of living in an RV are just as important as eating, sleeping, and washing. Will people get in one another's way? What about dressing? Will the cook be separated from the main activity while she's fixing the food? One family interviewed discovered while they were still renting that their floor plan gave them a closed-in feeling that was depressing. When they bought, they went for a plan that gave them an open feeling and used curtains as dividers for privacy.

DESIGN DETAIL

Manufacturers know that people go for any sort of special feature. For instance, one family picked the bar as the deciding factor when they selected their unit. The point was that all the units they saw had basically the same equipment and plan. In their case, the bar was the added attraction that made the sale.

There are some new designs in dinettes that have attracted the attention of the RV public. Dinette designs come right out of the boat builders' bag of tricks. Converting the table into a bed is a real space saver—but the bed shouldn't be advertised as being roomy enough for two adults. At first many makers used a center-post table. When the table was converted into a bed, the post and its base became a nightly storage problem. That has been corrected, and now the dinette has been taken one step further. The seat that faces backward while the table is in use can be swung around to face the road ahead so that occupants can converse with the driver and the person to his immediate right. It's like having a car with two back seats plus the added attraction of a place to nap in the rear. This is good design.

Traditionally, the industry has built the appliances against the walls. They are breaking away, to some extent, from this concept and finding that small spaces can be opened up. The picture of the kitchen turned into the aisle is a perfect example. Now the cooking area is part of the social setting. Compare that to the picture showing the corridor effect. And on the practical side, which of these floor plans would be easier to air-condition?

Left: In this RV the cook is part of the social group. Design in right-hand photo is too chopped up. The designer forgot that people are social.

The problem with RV designers is that they compartmentalize the units into three facets of living—eating, sleeping, bathroom needs —but seem to forget the social needs of people. We have come to do a lot of entertaining in our motor home. We can do it in our present unit. The first night we had our twenty-foot unit we threw a dinner party for eight. I do admit that the butler had difficulty serving, but we had a good cozy time. If you think you will be entertaining, you should make sure that you have seating space to make your guests comfortable.

Another example of a designer thinking only about eating, sleeping, and bathing. Unit shown above has no place for group activity. Picture below shows an open feeling, makes a good social center.

RUGS AND CARPETS

If carpeting comes optionally, steer away from it, and especially from shag rugs.

Carpet is often laid before cabinets are installed, so it is impossible to remove. Your unit can be delivered with a tile floor at no extra cost. Save the fifty dollars and take the tile. Spend the money for a good grade of indoor-outdoor carpeting and install it yourself. We did it in three pieces in our unit. Do not cement it down over the tile floor. Cut exactly to size, a very easy job with a mat knife. The better grade of carpet has a rubber back and will stay put.

The advantage to all this is obvious. If you spill something you can really clean it up. You'll be able to get to the tile floor underneath and clean it, too. Take the sections of carpet out of the unit

By installing your own rugs you can remove them for cleaning. Take them out when you have a garage mechanic in. Make a place in bad weather where guests can take off their shoes and keep the rugs dry.

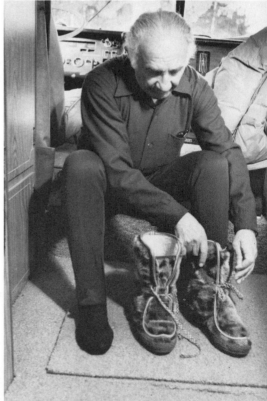

and clean them on the lawn or in the house. We use a foam spray, Johnson's Glory Spray Foam Cleaner. It's fast and easy. With the carpet out you can give the floor a fast cleaning before you put it back.

Place an extra piece of carpet at the door so that it gets all the dirt in bad weather.

A spare scrap of carpet is also good under the driver's feet. All motor homes come with the driving area carpeted. The scrap will keep clean that area where most wear occurs. We also put a piece over the motor housing. That becomes the tablecloth when we eat while driving.

There is another advantage to removable carpeting in a motor home. When the unit is left at the garage for a motor check the carpet is rolled up and put out of the way. Then oily footprints or greasy tools won't produce a problem.

When we decided to handle the carpet problem this way, we thought we would use boat snaps to keep the corners from curling up. They were not necessary. The thick rubber backing holds down very well. In cold country we put newspaper under the carpet as added insulation . . . it works fine.

In the well of the step, just inside the door, we carry two rugs. The bottom one is a piece that matches the main carpet. It's cut to the exact size of the well. On top of that we carry a fiber doorstep mat. It's thick and good for wiping feet. When we're parked we put it outside on the ground. Usually people see it and don't have to be asked to clean their shoes before they enter. It, too, is cut to fit the well so that it's no problem when traveling.

In ski country or in bad muddy conditions we make a place near the door for people to take off their boots. They can walk around on the carpet in stocking feet. We do try to keep the carpet dry. Even in the worst of cold weather it's a snug feeling to walk around on a warm, dry carpeted floor. Guests really don't mind.

We even put a bath mat outside the bathroom when someone is taking a shower. That's pretty fancy camping, but it does keep the rug dry. Some RVers use a remnant of carpet in the bathroom. It's nice on the feet when you use the bathroom in the middle of the night, and it's easy to remove when you take a shower.

Two kinds of ovens are available, above or below the counter.

MAN'S BEST FRIEND, THE STOVE

There is no question that on first glance the cooking stove in a modern motor home is a very attractive and efficient appliance. Ours is of the top wall-oven variety. It's easy to use and to keep clean. It has a lot of chrome and stainless steel that will shine up like new in nothing flat. I have a few words to say, however, about certain problems in using it. I would like to know who designed the power vent outlet. It works extremely well for demonstration purposes in a showroom. All you do is open the fan door over the oven and the fan starts automatically. But the door on the outside must be opened to let the exhaust air out. To reach this vent door from the outside one has to be a center on a basketball team. It's nine feet off the ground.

If this vent door is not latched while driving it'll flop and bang all the way down the road. The solution to this whole problem is to line the inside edge of the vent door with foam weather-stripping. If you use the kind that has adhesive on one side, the job will take only a matter of minutes. Then the door will never have to be latched and the fan will blow it open when it's in use. It'll save you the trouble of going outside to open it when it's raining, and it won't clang when you're on the road.

A better solution to the problem of the high vent is to put a throttle handle and cable on the inside and connect it to the vent door. Then you'll be able to open and close it at will. O.K., Mr. Designer?

The stove works well, and the oven will bake as well as Grand-mother's. The real problem is that it was never designed for a motor home. It was designed for a trailer . . . and there is a difference. When you are on the road with a trailer no one is in the unit as it rolls down the road, so what's the difference how much noise it makes? That is not true in a motor home; there all the parts, pilot tubes, burners and trays should be secured. Our Coleman stove sings and chirps like a flock of birds as we travel. This is very annoying because it can out-sing either my tape or the radio. The rougher the road, the louder it sings.

This stove vent could be opened only by a basket-ball player. Strange that the designers didn't think of that.

77

The cure has not proved simple. But here is the way to start. The stove has a pilot-light system just like our stove at home, and that's part of the trouble. The pilot is in the center, and telescoping tubes feed each burner. They sit in place until you start the engine, then they jump and rattle all over the place. Before you get where you are going, they fall out of their slots and roll around the bottom of the stove. So, when you stop, first thing you have to do is lift the stove top, rummage around to find the parts, put them together and then back in place. But there is a solution. Wire the parts in place. It will take only about five minutes to do the job. It's a shame that Mr. Coleman hasn't thought to do this little job for us. Thin copper wire will do the job. Wire the tubes to the burners and to the cross supports in the stove.

This is only a small part of the job, because the rest of the structure will still chirp. I admit that I still have not completely quieted my stove and I've been working on it for months. It seems that the only way to do it is by getting a little drunk. Here is how. After you drink a bottle of wine, save the cork. Then cut the cork into wedge-shaped wafers and wedge them between all the metal parts. After a few good wine parties you may lick this problem. If I sound a little rough on the stove manufacturers, I mean to sound that way. There is no stove on the market, as of this writing, that is quiet.

A roasting pan is supplied with the oven. Instead of fitting into a spring-pressure seat, it just sits in the oven and jounces around. I solved this problem by keeping it wrapped in a dish towel. This is a good example of a manufacturer making a product and never using it himself. If they had let Mrs. Coleman live in a motor home for a week, these problems would have been solved quickly.

I have one more complaint against propane cooking stoves. All other gas appliances in the motor home have thermostatically controlled shut-off valves. When the flame is extinguished the gas is shut off automatically. Not so in the stove. If a child played with the burner, or if a valve leaked, you could have raw gas escaping. We have solved this problem by putting a shut-off valve on the main supply pipe line. The valve is installed so that all you have to do is lift the top tray of the stove and the valve is easily reached.

The arrow points to the valve we installed as a shut-off point in the propane system. It's not provided by the stove makers; it should be.

All this may sound as though I were dissatisfied with the stove. It took some work on my part, but now it's really a fine stove. My wife enjoys it, and that's what really counts. It just seems a shame that the consumer has to finish the manufacturer's job to make it something you can live with when it's not heating the vittles.

One purpose of this book is to tell you how to use your appliances. I draw the line as far as the stove is concerned. I can cook a mean can of beans and scramble a fine egg. That's the end of it. All I can really suggest is that you will find the oven a fine place to store bread and cake while you travel. Actually, anything you can cook at home you can cook in an RV kitchen. A full-course dinner is no problem. You can broil, roast, bake, sauté, simmer, stew, or fry. If you can do it at home you can do it on the road.

Many stoves have the oven below the burners. These are good units. Be sure to order a hood, exhaust fan, and cooking light; they are options worth having. A good Christmas stocking gift for your wife is a flint-spark gun or a butane pipe lighter for lighting the stove. It won't give off the sulphur smell that the long wooden stove matches produce. My wife taught me a trick that other wives most likely know, but here it is anyway. Take sheets of aluminum foil and lay them on the floor of the stove, under the burners. If anything boils over the clean-up job will be simple. Just change the foil.

The oven makes a fine place to store bread. We have to wrap the oven pans in dish cloths to keep them quiet. Why didn't the designer think of metal clips to do this?

The beginning of a four-course dinner. Tent camping was never like this.

When refrigerators work, I can say some pretty hot things about them; when they don't the language can be rather cool. All RV refrigerators are absorption types and most of them give constant trouble. This industry needs a spanking: absorption-type refrigerators have been manufactured longer than any other type and should be trouble-free unless corners are cut to save costs. Absorption refrigerators have no moving parts. The only requirement is that the refrigerator sit level, because it depends on gravity to function. Wherever RVers congregate and start inspecting one another's units, they ask "How's your refrigerator?" before they swap names. I've had one refrigerator that never gave a bit of trouble in the eight years that it had been operating, while another was replaced three times within a year.

Refrigeration in this day and age is a science; all the answers are known. In an interview, the director of the largest supplier of units for the RV industry admitted that the problem was strictly cost. The engineers were sent back to the drawing board and told to find a way to cut corners so they could keep the price competitive. They did, but they also almost ruined the product.

I only wish I could list the refrigerators that are reliable today. Such a list might change from year to year. But this tip could be worth the price of this book—make the dealer from whom you buy the vehicle guarantee that he will replace the refrigerator if it does not work. Tell him that I said in my book to get it in writing. A bad refrigerator can ruin a vacation.

You may be reading this with alarm. Remember, I didn't say that all refrigerators are no good. I am saying the failure rate is higher than it should be. If your unit will operate for more than two months without a problem, you've got it made. If you do have a problem after that, it'll most likely be minor. A good cleaning or flame adjustment will put you back in business.

I can assure you that major repairs by your local authorized dealer are a waste of your time. The company director hit the nail on the head when he said that the industry has cut too many corners to make the price competitive. But the poor mechanic doesn't know that. He will look at a unit and say that the wiggima-jig is defective and they'll have to send to the factory for a new one. May I prove my point by quoting from a service bulletin sent to every authorized dealer for one large company:

> WITH THE BUSY SEASON COMING UP WE HAVE SOME GOOD FACTS YOU MAY BE INTERESTED IN KNOWING ABOUT ITEMS RETURNED AS DEFEC- TIVE LAST YEAR: EIGHT OUT OF TEN THERMO- COUPLES ARE NOT DEFECTIVE; OVER 50% OF THE HEATING ELEMENTS RETURNED ARE GOOD; SEVEN OUT OF TEN COOLING UNITS ARE GOOD.

In my book, those are bad facts, not good ones. It shows that the service people in the field don't know what they are doing and that the manufacturer had better redesign the heating element.

TIPS AND A SAGA

Let me tell you a story that will make you cry. But you'll learn a few tips that will make it all worthwhile. First, some background. Engineers design exact blueprints for construction of the compart-ment and chimney for refrigerators. RV manufacturers follow these specifications, since the venting of an absorption refrigerator is most important.

I met a fellow RVer from California who told me this story. He had constant blowout of the refrigerator's gas flame while traveling. This has been a common complaint; most RVers have run into it. Some units just seem to be susceptible to a passing truck. The flame is sucked out.

The Californian had a very large refrigerator; it was an eight-footer with a freezer on top. When he complained that he wanted the refrigerator replaced, after having tried all sorts of things to solve the blowout problem, he was told that it couldn't be done. The refrigerator was so big it wouldn't go through the door of his motor home. His unit had been built around it; the refrigerator was put in before the walls were assembled. That's tip number one. Anything bigger than a six-footer could give you such a problem . . . check it out before you buy.

That's only the beginning of this saga. He kept losing food and spending money as he traveled across the country. He said he lay awake at night trying to figure it out. Then the answer came to him. He had just stopped for gas and checked the flame; it was fine. Two things happened as he pulled out of the gas station. First the kids started fighting about whether or not the window should be opened . . . and a truck passed. Being as gun-shy as he was about trucks, he immediately stopped to check the flame. It was out. Then he put two and two together. When another truck had passed before he went into the gas station it hadn't disturbed the flame, yet with the window open the next truck sucked it out. He thought he'd solved his refrigerator problem! By keeping all the windows closed, he would never have flame blowout again. But now a new problem appeared. With the windows closed the family sweltered in the heat.

This man had a twenty-seven-foot unit with a small, 2500-watt generator that operated one air-conditioner. It wasn't big enough with the windows closed while traveling on the hot roads, so he made the big decision. He replaced his $700 generator with a bigger, $1200 one and installed a second air-conditioner for over $500. Now all his problems were solved at a total cost of about $1600, without counting the lost food.

Meanwhile, back at the ranch, where they manufactured his unit, the mechanic in charge of repairing refrigerators in the Customer Service Department was also losing sleep about this problem. He finally convinced his boss to let him take a unit with a refrigerator blowout problem on a vacation so he could try to work this thing out. The boss agreed, but not before he jokingly told the mechanic that he knew he was going to buy ice and just have a free vacation.

For years mechanics have been trying to solve the problem of the passing truck by building baffles around the flame, using spun-glass filters over the louvers on the refrigerator door, aluminum foil covers, etc., etc. This fellow decided that it wasn't the vacuum that trucks produced that sucked out the flame; it was being blown out. This could happen only if a leak through the refrigerator cabinet wall and an open window inside the motor home created a direct passage of air to the outside. Closed windows, he reasoned, would operate as a pressure seal. To test his theory, he opened the windows and sealed the wall joints of the refrigerator cabinet with three-inch cloth tape. The blowout problem was solved.

As the mechanic told the story, tears rolled down the Californian's cheeks. His refrigeration problem had been cured with eight cents worth of tape, a loss of about $1599.92.

Credit for sealing the compartment really goes to the Winnebago executive who had enough foresight to let his worker use the RV. Most industries give only the executives fringe benefits.

WHAT SHOULD A REFRIGERATOR DO?

First, you need to have a decent thermometer so you can determine the true readings in your refrigerator. The fifty-nine-cent ones from the local hardware store are useless; the old-style mercury-in-glass jobs are reliable.

The coldest reading should be in the freezing compartment, while maintaining a shelf temperature of between 40 and 50 degrees. A good example would be $+2$ degrees in the freezer and $+40$ shelf temperature. That's better than $+18$ in the freezer and $+25$ in the shelf; $+25$ will freeze your food. There is a temperature control adjustment that will have to be changed as the outside temperature fluctuates.

GET ON THE LEVEL

To make your refrigerator work well, your unit must be level. This sometimes becomes a problem. Why don't manufacturers stand the refrigerators on screw-type adjustable legs? Actually, the whole vehicle should be level. It's difficult cooking on an off-level stove. What about sleeping or walking? Same thing.

84

Mounting the circular level on the steering column makes the job so much easier for the driver.

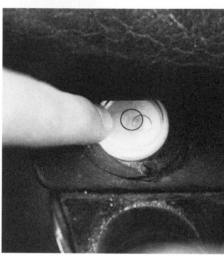

A circular level is supplied with the refrigerator. Manufacturers suggest the way to use the level is to place it in the freezer compartment. Then move the vehicle until the bubble is in the center of the level. Try this on a hot day and you could lose all your cool air from the box. This is really a poorly conceived procedure. Not only is it bad to keep the doors open so long, but ice on the floor of the freezing compartment would not permit you to get a true reading.

An easier and more accurate method is to use a second circular level. It can be obtained in a hardware store for a few cents. While the refrigerator is turned off, with no ice in the freezing compartment, place one of the levels in the box. Take the second level and mount it permanently near the steering wheel of the vehicle. Use

85

shims to get the one mounted near the wheel to read exactly like the one in the freezing compartment. Now the driver can see when the box is level without opening the doors and losing the cold air. It's easy: set up the chocks, drive on them and watch the bubble.

HOW DO YOU LEVEL A UNIT?

There are all sorts of devices on the market for leveling your unit; the magazines are full of them. Trailers are easy; you have only to worry about side-to-side level, because the front-and-back can be adjusted with the wheel on the tongue. Campers and motor homes present a more difficult problem.

Some units have hydraulic jacks on each corner. They're expensive, but they work fine. Ramps can be made or bought. I've seen automobile bumper jacks used. Two of them will do the job. Attach them and lift the body of the vehicle off its springs. This will also keep the unit from swaying while the kids are having a rock concert in the lounge.

AND TALKING ABOUT JACKS

While talking about jacks . . . some manufacturers have the nerve to supply a screw-up jack with the vehicle for changing a tire. My first experience many years ago with one of these gadgets caught me in the middle of desert country in Arizona. The weight was too much and the gears stripped before I got the wheel off the ground. Try that in the middle of August in the desert. The lesson

The truck body has to be raised a few inches in order to get the tire out of the wheel well. The extra jack is not provided. You can get one at a junk yard.

here is two-fold. A hydraulic jack is a must. Carry a heavy iron plate to set the jack on; it'll give the jack a solid base. Soft dirt on the shoulder could get you in trouble. Practice going through the mechanics of changing a tire to see what your problems are before you get caught with your wheel down. You will most likely discover that if you try to remove a rear tire you can't get it out of the wheel well. The body of a motor home usually has to be raised on its springs to get the tire out. Manufacturers seem to forget this. They supply an axle jack but no body jack. Go to an auto junkyard and

buy a used bumper jack. Then, when you raise the axle, put the bumper jack under the body and raise it.

There are all kinds of ramps that can be bought or made for leveling. They are usually bulky affairs and are trouble to carry. For ten years I've managed well with a few assorted lengths of wooden planks. The boards can be made into ramps or just used as platforms. They're easy to stow. You can always find a spot where you only have to worry about two wheels.

A tip: refrigeration engineers say that side-to-side level of a refrigerator is more critical than front-to-back.

There is an electrical device available that shows when the vehicle is level. It's a box mounted on the dash. Four corner lights, one for each of the rig's wheels, indicate which corner or side is low. But be careful not to get gadget-happy. The level will do the job just as well, and not much can go wrong with it.

WHAT SIZE BOX?

The size of the refrigerator you select should be determined by the number of people who are going to live in your unit and what kind of eaters they are. The big mistake most women make is being infatuated with the large boxes. As we have already said, the giant sizes can produce a repair problem because they can't be removed from the RV if need be.

It's better to store food in a compact manner than allow it to slide all around the shelves. We did very well with a two-and-one-half-cubic-foot unit for many years. When we went to a bigger motor home the four-cubic-foot box was sheer luxury. When Olive considered the six-cubic-foot box for four adults, she decided the extra cabinet space above the refrigerator was more important to her.

HOW TO PACK FOOD

The secret of the small box is in the way it's packed. There are a number of gadgets on the market to aid compact packing. For instance, there are snap-on railings that fit on the front of the

88

The secret is to open and shut the refrigerator quickly. Plastic boxes make this possible; they also keep things from spilling and rattling.

shelves to prevent items from sliding out when the door is opened. We've tried them, and they're more trouble than they're worth. The answer to all the problems of spillage, accessibility, and speed is plastic boxes of varying size. Items are grouped by size and type of packaging. Instead of holding the door open and rummaging around for one item, the pastic box containing that item can be removed quickly. When traveling, things won't skid around or make noise if they are in the plastic boxes. A six-pack of beer is set on the lid of a plastic box. This keeps the beer in place and prevents it from rattling.

There is another worthwhile trick: we place a strip of contact paper on the door behind the stand-up bottles and cans. This cuts out noise and prevents the tops of the containers from scarring the plastic interior.

We have a rule. The door of the refrigerator must be locked when closed, even if we are parked. This rule develops a habit and will prevent grief when you start up and are going around your first curve.

On a very hot, muggy summer day the outside refrigerator

compartment service door should be propped open with a stick. This allows more air flow to cool the coils. If, in your unit, this outside door is screwed in place, it should be changed to a hinge system. This will simplify getting air to the coils.

A stick will hold the refrigerator service door open and give all the ventilation needed on a muggy day. Why waste money on an awning?

WATER, WATER EVERYWHERE . . . WE HOPE

Our first recreation vehicle carried twelve gallons of water, and what a real luxury it was. Ounce by ounce, we drew it off with a hand-operated galley suction pump, and nary a drop was wasted. Today's fifty- to seventy-gallon tanks make us feel guilty as we go back and read what Captain Randolph Marcy had to say in his 1859 journal about getting and storing water:

> Drinking water may be obtained during a shower from the drippings from a tent or by suspending a cloth or blanket by the four corners and hanging a small weight to the center, so as to allow all the rain to run towards one point, from hence it drops into a vessel beneath. If wooden kegs are used they must frequently be looked after, and soaked, in order that they may not shrink and fall to pieces.

There are two basic water systems used in modern RV units: the air-pressure and electric-pump types. The pressure system is air-tight. An air pump attached to the system builds up air pressure in the tank and forces the water into the pipes. The pump builds the pressure up to about forty-five pounds and then shuts itself off. When you open the faucet the air pressure forces the water out. When the amount of water in the tank is reduced, the air pressure is also reduced. The air pump will automatically come on when the pressure drops to about twenty-five pounds. The flow of water is even.

The electric-pump system is similar to a galley pump. Water flows into the pump by gravity and is then pumped on demand to the faucet. When the faucet is turned on the electric pump is also turned on. The flow of water is in spurts. The pressure system is considered the better of the two and is used in the finer units.

When we graduated from our galley pump system to our first pressure system, we had the option of thirty or sixty gallons of water. If twelve could last as long as it did, we figured that thirty would give us enough for swimming. How wrong we were! The air-pressure and electric-pump systems are a great convenience, but they eat up water as if they were sponges. Take all the water options the manufacturer offers—it'll pay off in hot showers—and remember Captain Marcy who got his water in dry stream beds by sinking flour barrels in the sand near cottonwood trees.

You may shave at home by running the water throughout the whole agonizing process. Not so in a motor home; an inch or so of hot water in the basin will do just as good a job on your face. Don't turn on both cold and hot to blend the mixture. Turn on only the hot. Catch the first water that comes through the pipes; it'll be cool. As the hot water works through the pipes, use it to bring the temperature up to where you want it. You'll be surprised how much water this can save. Unless you are hooked up to city water or your trip is for only a weekend, you will have to learn the foregoing way to use water. This is very often difficult to teach to small children. Since I raised such a fuss about the water with my kids, I'll understand if they become alcoholics.

You are bound to waste water with an electric-pump or air-pressure system. The flow from an air-pressure system is as strong as the one in your home. The motor-driven air pump is a reliable little gadget but if it fails the only way you'll get at your water is to drain it out of the main tank. A tip: carry an ordinary tire or bicycle pump. It can be attached to the "tire" valve that's incorporated in the pressure system. Pump in air and you'll get water. This'll take care of you until you get the pump repaired. Some suggest using the air at a gasoline station for this purpose. It'll do the trick fast, but stations seldom keep their compressors clean. You could get a bad taste in your water. Never put too much pressure in the system. Forty to forty-five pounds will do everything you'll need and it won't blow out a joint and cause a leak.

Electric-pump systems are reliable, but if the pump should fail there isn't much you can do. Some RVs have a galley pump in the system for just such an emergency. Galley pumps have a habit of losing their suction. It's a good idea to keep a few ounces of water handy in a plastic bottle for priming them. There is nothing so frustrating as having forty gallons of water in a tank and not being able to get at it for want of a few ounces to prime the pump. You prime it by pouring the few ounces of water into the pipe. Then pump and the suction will draw the water.

Although we talk about winter use of the water system elsewhere, there are two good tips to remember. First, don't forget to empty the water from the pump when you drain the system. This, of course, is not necessary in a pressure system. But there is a second little trick to remember with this type: the external air valve on these units sits facing up; keep a valve cover on it during the winter, or water that sits in the rim of the valve will freeze.

WATER, WATER EVERYWHERE AND NOT A DROP TO DRINK

We Americans have taken our water for granted in both quality and quantity, but we are learning fast. With all the progress we have made in this country, water pollution is upon us. Captain Marcy had a few words to say about water back in 1859, but his problem was extraordinary . . . ours is commonplace.

Water taken from stagnant pools with putrid vegetable matter and animalculae would be very likely to generate fevers and dysenteries if taken into the stomach without purification. Therefore it should be thoroughly boiled, and by mixing powdered charcoal with it the disinfecting process is perfected. Water may be purified by placing a piece of alum in the end of a stick that has been split, and stirring it around in a bucket of water. Charcoal and the leaves of prickly pear are also used for the same purpose.

Possibly we should use the captain's prickly pear leaves and alum stick in our cities today. How has it happened that a nation that once led the world in public health and sanitation is now faced with so serious a water pollution problem? Public health estimates show that eighty percent of our water is in some way polluted or contaminated, and you can no longer rely on some unseen agency to insure your health. You would think that once we get away into the country the water would be of better quality, but it's not. Testings have shown that even the clear water we find in our campsites is often inferior. Twenty years ago, upstate New York water was considered the best in the nation. Just last summer we had to start buying water at sixty-three cents a gallon in order to have coffee fit to drink.

If you are lucky and have good water at home, that doesn't mean you'll be free of problems in your RV even if you use home water in it. RVs have a special problem that must be watched in the summer. Heat from the sun and road can raise the temperature in the water tank and start bacterial action. The water system is under air pressure. Airborne bacteria will multiply rapidly as the temperature increases. However, generally this is not a health hazard.

FLUSH THE SYSTEM

Once every year your water tanks should be flushed. Pour four teaspoons of concentrated household detergent into the tanks for every ten gallons of water. This can be done by putting it in the hose before it's connected, if you do not have a screw cap so that it can be poured in directly. Add the water, let it sit, then run the soapy water full-force out of the system. Rinse it all out well with clean water. After you get all the detergent out, add a very concentrated solution of household chlorine bleach—a cup for every ten gallons of water. Open the faucets to draw the bleach into the pipes, close them again, and let the bleach stand for half an hour. Be sure you get a distinct chlorine smell each time the taps are opened. Flush the whole system very well.

TREAT THE WATER

Most people don't bother to treat their water unless they get into an area that they've been warned about. If they ever saw what they were drinking under a microscope, they'd go running for a bottle of Clorox. Health authorities recommend ordinary laundry bleach like Clorox, Purex, Sunburst, etc., for the treatment of water. It's easy to do. One teaspoon of bleach for every ten gallons of water will handle harmful bacteria, viruses, and slime-forming organisms. One of the problems is that you'll get a chlorine taste in the water. This can now be overcome in an RV with a water purification system. It's easy to install, or you can order one put in at the factory. It's a miniature of the process that the government recommends for our cities. First you put in enough chlorine to handle any amount of fluctuation in the contamination level, and after it's done its job you remove most of the chlorine to get rid of the taste. A water purification system does all this for you. It also filters the water, removing dirt, unpleasant tastes, and odors. The cost to operate it is less than two cents a gallon.

SOME TIPS

When you start flushing or treating your water system, open the taps to prevent back pressure. If you have a two-tank pressure system and are treating the water chemically, close the air-pressure release valve when the tanks are about half-full. Let the hose con-

94

tinue to run and build up pressure. This will equalize the water across the two tanks and carry the chemicals into each tank. If the tanks are being filled by hand the pressure pump will accomplish the same thing.

It's good to carry your own hose for filling the fresh water tanks. If you use one at a gas station, wipe off the fitting. Goodness only knows where they have dragged it! If your hose is plastic, flush it out before using. The plastic has a way of imparting a strange taste. Never use the hose or water provided at a sewer dumping station for filling the tanks. That hose is for washing down only. If you have any other problem, put some bourbon in the water and drink to Captain Marcy.

TOILETS

The john in the motor home has put more families on the road than any other one appliance. The shower may rate number two. The modern, compact bathrooms in RV units are truly luxurious and have very little in common with the usual ideas about camping. Many people I've questioned do not use the john in a self-contained unit exclusively. It's best to consider it as a reserve. Rest stops while traveling are still in order. There is no reason to use tank space when clean rest rooms are easily available. Often when one is parked, rest room facilities are only a short distance away, but at night and other times having your own on board is a real comfort.

TWO BASIC FLUSH SYSTEMS

The two basic flush systems are the holding-tank and recycling types, or there may be a combination of both. The holding-tank type comes as a standard equipment with the unit. It consists of a flushing stool mounted on a Fiberglas holding tank (marine type). Fresh water from the pressure system washes the bowl when it's flushed. The holding tanks contain about thirty gallons. Special chemicals control the odor and keep the bowl sanitary. There is very little that can go wrong with this system and these units use very little fresh water.

The recycling toilets are smaller versions of the ones used in commercial jets. You fill these systems with about four gallons of water when you start out. This is all the water the toilet uses for fifty to eighty flushings. Grinders and filters are incorporated in the unit, which runs off the 12-volt electrical system. Chemicals keep the water fresh. Antifreeze keeps it running in the winter. When the charge has been used up, it's dumped into the holding tank, more chemicals and water are put in, and the cycle is ready to start all over again.

Both of these systems use the holding tank, and it has to be emptied at a dumping station. Listings of these stations are compiled each year by Woodall Publishing Company. Your dealer will carry them.

96

Gas stations are starting to install dumping stations to attract the RV public. The water nearby is only for washing down the hose and valves.

Emptying the holding tank is not as difficult as it might seem. I have made an improvement in my unit and think manufacturers should incorporate it into their systems. In the meantime, you can do it, or have your dealer do it for you.

In all makes, the system is emptied by using a flexible sewer hose. It's connected to the clean-out trap on the holding tank and put into the dumping station pipe. The valve is opened, and the holding tank is emptied. The whole toilet system is then flushed with clean water. In some makes, the connecting of the hose to the clean-out trap can be a dirty chore and manufacturers suggest you use rubber gloves. The extra valve we installed does away with all these problems and the gloves.

Here is the way it works. (If you study the drawing as you read this, it will become very clear.) The holding tank can be used for both the sewage from the john and the water drained from the sinks and shower. If it is used only for the sewage from the john, there is no problem when emptying the holding tank. The valve labeled "original valve" holds the sewer back until the dumping hose is connected. When all is ready the original valve is opened and the tank empties. If the holding tank is being used only for the john, water from the sinks bypasses it. The cap is removed from the end of the clean-out trap and the sink water flows out directly onto the ground or into a collecting bucket.

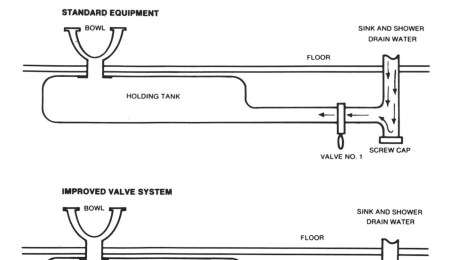

The problem *(top drawing)* is to remove the screw cap to empty the holding tank containing a mixture of sink and sewer water. Even when valve No. 1 is closed to hold back the main flow until the cap is removed and the hose connected, the dirty water held between the cap and valve No. 1 will soil the hands when the cap is removed. By installing valve No. 2 *(lower diagram)* the system can be controlled by the valves, making the job clean.

98

It's a different story if the holding tank is going to be used for both sewage and sink water. Then the clean-out trap cap is closed by screwing it in place. The original valve is opened. The water from the john is still held in the holding tank. The water from the sink is held in the pipe by the cap. As more sink water comes down the pipe, it backs up, passing through the open original valve and then into the holding tank. Now when you empty the holding tank you must close the original valve and connect the hose onto the clean-out end. To do this you have to unscrew the cap and take it off. The water that is held between the original valve and the cap is a mixture of sewer and sink water . . . not very nice to handle while unscrewing the cap. Our added valve eliminates all the problems. You can forget the cap if you like. The transfer of flow is now all handled by valves, and your hands never get wet.

When buying an RV, check the drain and sewage system; if they work the way we have just described, have the added valve installed.

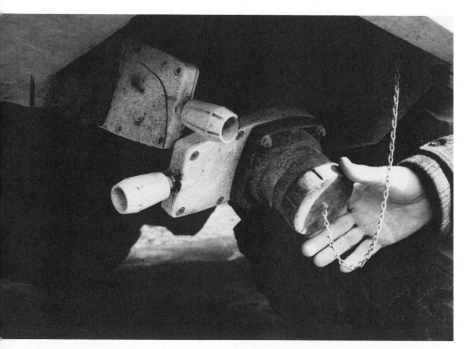

The upper valve is the original equipment. We added the second valve to the system, just behind the cap. Emptying is now a clean job.

There is another product that could revolutionize the whole waste problem. It's called Thermasan. It incinerates all wastes—liquid and solid—in a section of the engine's exhaust manifold. You control this at the dashboard of the vehicle. While you're cruising down the highway, a switch controlling a pump begins to inject the contents of the holding tank into the incinerator, which they call a sanitizer. The wastes are consumed by the 2000-degree automotive exhaust. Solids are pulverized, the odor-producing materials are altered by the heat, and the liquids are evaporated. Solids and liquids are burned into an odorless, non-polluting, bacteria-free gas. Thermasan meets all federal emission and health codes.

This system works only when the vehicle is going thirty miles an hour or faster. It'll consume about five gallons of waste per hour. It won't work while the unit is parked or the engine is idling, nor will it work while driving in slow city traffic. If you are going to be parked a long time, the system can be emptied in the conventional manner with the sewer hose. It's a fine system; its price is its only drawback.

How does one decide on which john? Money may be an important consideration. The marine type comes as standard equipment. The recycling, jet type costs about two hundred dollars more and the Thermasan costs about seven hundred dollars. Also consider the age of the children in the family and whether or not other facilities are going to be available most of the time. After questioning many RVers on this matter, I tend to stay with the original standard marine toilet, because very little, if anything, can go wrong with it. I found the answers from most people support this decision. They are happy with what they have gotten used to . . . except for those who have had mechanical problems that required servicing.

How safe is liquid propane (LP) gas? The answer is obvious. If it were dangerous we wouldn't be allowed to use it for our stoves, furnaces, and refrigerators. Experimental automobiles are now being run on propane. The engineers claim it's safer than gasoline. We're going to see more of this in the future because the emission from an engine run on LP is eighty percent less than from a gasoline engine.

Accidents involving bottled gas are rare, but when one does occur it is serious. I've seen the results of only one such accident, and the motor home was a mess. The trouble did not involve the two tanks stored in the unit's compartment, but it did involve extra tanks that were being transported loose inside the vehicle. These bottles had just been filled and were being taken home for storage as a future convenience. On the trip from the LP station they stood in the aisle of the motor home. One bottle fell over, the valve was damaged, and gas escaped. The driver stopped short and ran back to get that tank outside. He must have set off a spark with his shoe. The explosion blew the wall out, injuring the driver. The moral of the story is plain: handle bottles carefully.

HOW DO YOU PREVENT TROUBLE?

You'll know if you're having an LP problem. When the gas is manufactured, a chemical that smells like garlic is incorporated in it. Even if you have a small leak you'll notice the smell. The odor is not detected when the gas is burned in normal operation.

How do you prevent problems? For one thing, before you purchase a vehicle, make sure that it provides a way to secure the gas tanks in their outside compartment. This is such a basic necessity that you might wonder why it is mentioned. Well, incredible as it may seem, units have been made without this feature. If the tanks are not secured, their vibration as they bounce around will finally fatigue the copper connecting tube and cause a high-pressure leak.

Secondly, once or twice a year the whole gas system should be carefully checked. All connections should be tightened and the appliances should be cleaned with a vacuum cleaner. After a prolonged period of storage, the burners should be inspected for dust and cobwebs. For some unknown reason, spiders love the smell of the gas or its residue, and if they build nests in the orifices you won't get a proper flame. If a pilot light won't work, the whole appliance won't function properly.

When the contents of the LP tank are getting low, you will notice the smell caused by the odor-producing chemical in the propane. At first this smell might send you scurrying to find a leak. It lasts for only a few minutes and is a signal that the tank is low.

Another problem with propane gas that sometimes arises is a leak outside of the unit. In this case you might never know it except that you finally come to notice that the LP consumption is high. You can check whether there is a leak by attaching a pressure valve to the system at the tanks. Many of the LP stations, however, do not have the right pressure-valve equipment for use in the tight confines of an RV's tank compartment.

Another way to detect LP gas leaks is to use a Fisher gauge. Many bottled-gas dealers have one. To use it, you first turn off all the gas appliances, making sure all the pilot lights are also out. Remove one of the burners from the stove. Attach the free end of the gauge hose to the spud from which the burner was removed, so that the gas will flow into the gauge. Turn that stove valve on and take a reading on the dial. Now turn off the main valve of each bottle so that no more gas will flow into the system. Watch the gauge indicator. If there is a loss of pressure, you have a leak; if it shows no loss in two or three minutes, your system is fine.

All appliances are set to operate on eleven inches of water-column pressure. Often when an appliance malfunctions the cause turns out to be incorrect gas pressure. The Fisher gauge can be used to see if the pressure is correct. To adjust the regulator, you remove the dust cap and turn the inner adjusting screw clockwise to increase the pressure and the opposite way to decrease it. But now let's see how you test for a suspected leak if this equipment is not available.

If there is an automatic change-over valve in your LP gas system, it will serve as a good, built-in leak detector. This accessory is a must for all units with two bottles. It costs only a few dollars, so buy this optional feature. During normal operations the valve will automatically switch from an empty tank to the full one to supply the appliance. It can save your food on a hot day while you are off swimming.

The valve has a flag device that shows red when the pressure in the line falls. This indicates that the first tank is empty and the full one is being used. It's time to get the first tank refilled. An arrow even shows which tank has been emptied. From the switching device the gas flows into a reducing valve. This valve receives the high pressure gas from the bottle and reduces its pressure before it travels through the pipes to the appliances. Bottled-gas experts say that the reducing valve, as it gets old, will not hold pressure indefinitely, but it will hold it long enough for our method of using it to test the system for leaks.

Here is how you do it. Turn off the main valve to each appliance. Turn on both bottles of gas at their main valve. The red flag will disappear. The window will show clear or white . . . gas is flowing and the pressure is up in the line. Now turn both main valves on the bottles off. Watch the window. The red flag will not show, and the window should stay clear for ten or fifteen minutes. If it slowly turns red, you have a leak. If the red flag shows in a minute your leak is a big one. You now know that the leak is between the reducing valve and the main valve of one of the appliances. If you find no leak, then test each appliance one at a time. Give them each the fifteen-minute red-flag check. (In the section on stoves we suggest that a main valve be installed, since manufacturers don't include it with the appliance.)

In addition, the valves at the main tanks should be tested with a heavy solution of soap and water. Use a small brush to paint the solution on. If there is a leak the soap will bubble up. The same can be done with all interior gas joints.

Where the gas pipes are routed outside, underneath the unit, a cigarette lighter can be used to make the test. This is on the low side of the reduction valve. If there is a leak, a blue flame will show up. This flame method *should not* be used if you can smell gas, nor should it be used to test the main tank valves.

This system of using the automatic switch-over valve for testing is a good one because you can run the check without any extra tools, wherever you are.

SOME HINTS

Propane or butane (which is rarely used nowadays) is available almost anywhere in the country. In cold country only use propane. It has a much lower freezing temperature than butane.

Because both these gases are heavier than air and fall to the floor, opening a window will not solve the problem of removing escaped gas from a unit. All of the appliances except the cooking stove have a shut-off valve that works automatically if the flame goes out. The stove does not have this! So don't let kids play with the knobs.

The connections at the main tank often cause problems. For one thing, they are hard to get at. Another problem is that they are made of brass, so if you use a wrench on them that does not make a snug fit you'll chew up the nut. These fittings have left-hand threads; all other fittings in the gas system have right-hand threads. But the access problem is the main one: the compartments for tanks are made so small that the tank just about fits. It is hard to put an ordinary wrench on the nut from the side, to loosen it, because tanks have a protective metal collar which gets in the way. The nut can be loosened easily from above, but that's impossible when the tank is in its compartment.

To get around this problem, I took an ordinary 7/8-inch box wrench and cut out enough so it would pass over the copper tube. The photograph will show clearly how this is done. The cutout was made with a hack saw, or it can be done with a file wheel on a drill press.

104

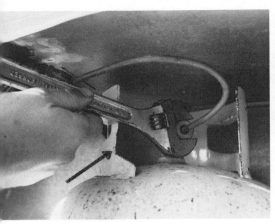

In the tight confines of its compartment, you cannot work on the tank from the top. Even with the protective collar cut away (arrow), an ordinary wrench cannot fit against the nut. The picture on the right shows what the problem is as seen outside the unit.

A box wrench is correctly shaped to get in and fit snugly against the nut. Part of the collar still has to be cut away. A section is cut out of the wrench so it will slip over the copper line (*right*). *Below:* An easy way to store the wrench while traveling.

ELECTRICAL SYSTEM

All modern units operate on both 12-volt direct current (DC) and 110-volt alternating current (AC) electricity. The self-contained 12-volt (DC) system consists of two parts. One battery handles the automotive requirements, and the other handles the living quarters. When the engine is shut off, the house current will automatically flow from one of these batteries. That way you will always have a live battery to start the vehicle.

When the engine is operating, a switch on the dash must be put on so the engine alternator will charge both batteries while moving. If a prolonged stay in one place is going to be made it's a good idea to run the engine with the dual switch on to build up the house battery. Many units have a battery-condition meter to show the state of each battery. This also should be referred to often. It's a good idea to carry an inexpensive hygrometer and check the battery water every few days during a prolonged stay.

Get the family used to turning out lights. Some fixtures have a switch that lights either one or two bulbs. Use the one-bulb system unless the extra light is required.

You can also plug the unit into the 110-volt current provided at campgrounds or from another outside source. This will save the use of the batteries. The electricity is passed through a converter which reduces the 110-volt AC current to 12-volt DC current for all the appliances that require it (lights, exhaust motor, furnace motor, etc.). The wall outlets in the unit carry 110-volt AC current, so you can plug into these outlets any 110-volt home appliance you wish.

Most converters also have a battery charger built in, so that when you are plugged in to 110-volt current you are also charging the batteries. The amperage of this charger is not usually very high. For example, it'll put in about what a fan will take out. Some owners wire in a second battery charger, in order to get a faster rate of charge.

If your converter has its own switching system, become familiar with its workings. With the switches in the wrong position, you would be plugged in to 110 volts but still working off the battery.

Built-in 110-volt power-generating plants provide the same conveniences as when you are plugged in to outside 110-volt current. To use the current from the generator, it's necessary to have the converter switch at the generator settings. Your generator, like any other motor, needs periodic maintenance. Manual instructions should be followed. It is important to watch the oil level in these units. It must be checked every eight hours of running time.

Electrical fires are rare in RV units, but you should have a plan in mind for such an emergency. Do not use water on an electrical fire. Foam extinguishers should be kept handy and all adults in the party should know how to operate them. As soon as the foam has the fire under control, the electric system should be disconnected at the battery and/or the plug-in. If two people are present, one should disconnect the electricity as the other uses the extinguisher.

TIPS

Carry an extra set of fuses. Make sure you have a selection of fuses of the necessary ampere ratings.

Extension cords for use in plugging into outside 110-volt current should be of the three-wire type, which includes a ground. A cord made of No. 12 wire will carry any load you will need . . . even for an air-conditioner.

It is smart to carry a variety of adapters with you, since the three-wire, outside hookups are not standard. Such a selection can be obtained at almost any good hardware store.

Carry a prewired electrical "Y," so that a single outside outlet can be shared with another vehicle if necessary.

Clamps on the posts of the large 220-amp house battery are for the charger, which is always hooked to one or the other battery. The 70-amp automotive battery is being tested.

WINTER LIVING

You may never take your recreation vehicle into cold weather. In fact, many people go the route of the RV so they can avoid the cold. Might I suggest, however, that you read this section on winter living even if you do expect only to bask in the sun. Severe cold can teach us much about how to use an RV; much can be learned in the bitter winter weather that can be helpful on roasting hot days.

Little tricks, such as keeping the curtains drawn on the windward side to make a dead air space between the curtains and glass, work just as well in the summer as in the winter. In the summer the curtains would be drawn on the sunny side to act as insulation.

Still more important is the system of back-ups that one has to have in the cold weather. Learning to use an RV successfully when the wind-chill factor is 40 below zero will prepare you for any problems you'll run into in any weather. Just as the astronauts have back-up systems for all the problems they face, you'll need the same approach, on a lesser scale, in your RV living. Cold climates are the place to learn what an RV is all about.

ONLY THE HARDY GO NORTH

Over Christmas vacation Santa and his bag were piled into the back of our motor home, and we were off to Grandmother's house in Virginia. On the way we played the usual game of counting rigs of different manufacture and type. The exact number is not important, but as we headed south our headlights were constantly blinking hello to all the units we passed. The further south we went the more RVs we saw. I had the urge to stop, call my broker, and tell him to buy RV stocks.

It was exactly the opposite story when we turned around and headed north to spend the New Year skiing in Vermont. Mile after mile, we never had to use the headlight switch. During our travels and stay in Vermont we didn't see even one other unit. Where was that colony of mobile skiers we expected to find parked at the foot of the Sugarbush slope? South!

This isn't too surprising when you think about it. Look at the literature most RV manufacturers present to the public—beach scenes, summer in the mountains, and so on. Today, dealers don't even know how their vehicles will perform in sub-zero weather.

Soon, that's all going to change. The ski market is too big to ignore, especially with the surge into cross-country skiing. Here is a sport that goes hand in glove with a motor home, because all ages can participate.

Officials of some of the biggest motor-home manufacturers suggest that in temperatures below freezing you not use the water system in your unit but instead carry five-gallon jerry cans. Before I'd do that, I'd go to a motel. Are they saying that if you live in the north you can only use your unit nine months a year? That's a lot of investment sitting idle for three months!

Protecting the fresh-water system is the most important problem in winterizing a house on wheels. A frozen copper water line could spell disaster. You'd be ice skating instead of skiing, and to repair the ruptured line you'd have to rip out a wall.

109

OPTIONS FOR WINTER

If you expect to take trips in your motor home into sub-zero weather areas, make it a point to tell your dealer so and arrange to include the necessary options when the unit is manufactured. It will be a lot cheaper and easier to install these features while the unit is being built than to try to add them later.

As of this writing, no manufacturer offers a complete winter package in a motor home . . . but it's coming. The outdoor writers—this one included—have strongly urged manufacturers to come up with the needed answers. My own unit is winterized, and that's why we had no qualms about heading north for the New Year. But it took us a long time to figure out all the difficulties one is going to face when the wind-chill factor is extreme. I can save you the time involved in anticipating the problems, if not the work of having the necessary modifications made.

TIRES FOR SNOW

Starting from the ground up, the first essential is proper tires. A survey made at the last national recreation-vehicle show revealed that more than fifty percent of the vehicles on display were not adequately shod for snow or mud. Manufacturers seem to accept whatever tires the chassis builder chooses to put on the unit. This is inexcusable. Mobility is the name of the game, and you should be able to drive your motor home off the highway and over the back country roads all year round. Don't be persuaded by the salesman that you won't have a problem because of all the weight you'll carry. Motor homes have been stuck in as little as five or six inches of wet snow. The belted radial tires are good, but mud and snow tires are even better. If they don't have studs, they can be used all year, and they're designed to run as comfortably on highways as the thinly grooved "fair-weather" tire.

One more point about tires. The rims will accept more than one size tire. Opt for the bigger size . . . it's safer. Before you drive off his lot, have the dealer put on the right tires—the biggest all-weather tires.

110

In a motor home you have two heating systems. The engine heater, for driving comfort, can be used in an emergency for general heat. With the engine at idle, and the blowers on full power, we've heated our unit in below-zero weather and it almost roasted us.

The main heating system, however, is the thermostatically controlled liquid-propane furnace. These forced-air systems are extremely efficient. They come with different outputs measured in British Thermal Units (Btus). If you are going into cold country, get one with the biggest output; it'll be an optional feature. It costs only a few more dollars to have the larger unit installed, and it's worth it. The usual thinking is that the larger size is a waste of money. The mathematics of it goes like this: to keep a room at 70 degrees F., the same amount of bottled gas will be consumed whether you use a 23,000-Btu unit or a 30,000-Btu unit. The difference, however, will be in the amount of time the heater runs. If it takes the smaller furnace five minutes to raise the temperature three degrees, and the larger unit can do it in three minutes (both consuming the same amount of gas), what's the real advantage of the extra cost of the bigger heater? The answer is not in gas consumption, it's in the electricity used to run the forced-air system. The motor that runs the blower uses 7 amps. All you have to do is run out of electricity some night when you are asleep . . . you'll wake up with a frozen unit. The shorter blower time will mean less consumption of electricity. What's more, battery output in cold weather is less than it is at normal temperatures. By all means, we advise taking the option of the bigger furnace.

BATTERY

Most modern units, as we noted earlier, have a dual battery system. This is not the case, however, with some of the small units. In cold weather it's essential that you have a double, separate-battery electrical system, even if it means having your dealer or mechanic put it in specially. Nothing could be more discouraging than finding out that one of the kids left the bathroom light on all night and you can't start the engine.

A 70-amp automotive battery is considered large. This is fine for engine power but not for the household living area, so opt for the bigger, 220-amp battery which is offered at an extra charge. The units normally come through with two 70s, but one 70 for the living area won't take you through a full night of running a heater on a ski slope, and it might not even be enough for a chilly night in the fall.

THE ELECTRICAL GENERATOR IN WINTER

Most RVers consider the built-in, 110-volt, electric power plant a must for the summer. It's the only way to have the luxury of air-conditioning on those hot, muggy days when you're not near an outside source of 110-volt power. In freezing weather, it is just as useful. It relieves the battery, provides a way of recharging it, and has some other uses, too, as you will see when we describe a typical winter day in an RV and how these optional features are used to operate in below-zero weather.

Generator systems producing 4000 and 5000 watts are available, as well as smaller ones. A 4000-watt system is powerful enough for most jobs. You'll have to go to a 5000-watt system, however, if you have more than one air-conditioner and expect to use a lot of other electrical appliances. Any unit smaller than the 4000-watt has the added disadvantage of being noisy. Our 4000 purrs us to sleep.

The electric generator is a very desirable option. It gives you the use of all the electrical appliances you have at home. It's very reliable, but you have to check the oil every eight hours.

Also important for winter motor-home living is the battery charger which is built into most of the converters and reduces the 110-volt AC current to 12-volt DC current, as described on pages 106–07. So find out two things. First, does your converter actually have the battery-charging feature? Some manufacturers save a few bucks by not installing this feature. Second, find out the rate of amperage output of the charger. If you use the 110-volt power plant and have a 12-volt motor running at the same time, your battery will receive no benefit, because your converter battery charger will be putting into the battery only what the motor is drawing out. There will be little or no net gain for the battery. In the winter, this is important, since you'll want to go at least all night on battery alone. Then you'll want to build the battery up the next day. There is an easy solution to this problem: install an extra auto-battery charger. An 8-amp charger that will also cut down and be a trickle charger can alleviate your electrical problems. It can be used in conjunction with the power plant or 110-volt hook-up.

ALTERNATOR AS A BACK-UP

You have another back-up system. The automotive alternator, as we have seen, will put out a good charge at idle speed. A word of advice here. Many units are being produced with only 40- or 45-amp alternators. When all appliances are on and running—wipers, driving air-conditioning, lights, radio—a 40- or 45-amp alternator won't have enough output to charge up the second battery. A motor home needs a 60-amp alternator; then you'll be on the safe side.

A valuable accessory that you can buy with the unit is called a battery-condition meter. This meter shows battery voltage. It's an inexpensive item and a good thing to have on the dash if you expect to spend a lot of time in cold areas. It'll save having to go outside to hook a meter onto the battery. Having it conveniently located inside the unit will pay off if somebody remembers to push the switch and take a reading before the lights start to go dim.

An interesting thing about lights going dim . . . it happens so gradually that very often you're out of electricity before you realize it. Train the family to speak up when they notice the lights dimming.

We always carry a hygrometer with us. It costs only a dollar. But I can almost tell what the reading of the battery water will be by keeping check on what the voltage regulator is doing while I drive. If your unit has only an "idiot light" to tell if you are charging or not, by all means install a voltage regulator.

HEAT LOSS

You don't have to be an engineer to know that your windows are the major problem in the transfer of the heat on the inside to the cold outside . . . and the reverse. This is really a twofold problem in more than one sense. Loss of heat is the problem we all know about. But there's another one connected with it—condensation. Water can ruin your interior woodwork. They say that a large oak tree will give off a ton of water in a day. Put a few people in a motor home, and also do your cooking there, and you'll be surprised how much water is put into the air. Three people sleeping in a unit can put up to a quarter-inch of ice on all the windows by morning. During the day, it melts off, and that's a lot of water dripping down on woodwork and cushions.

Some day the manufacturers will have enough sense to use thermo-glass and storm windows, or a combination of the two. This will not only help with the winter problems but in summer the double glass will keep the unit cool.

Manufacturers haven't wised up to that point yet, so before heading north we made our own storm windows. They were simple. We measured the interior aluminum frames of our windows and ordered one-eighth-inch plexiglass cut to the same size. Around the edge of the plastic we laid three-quarter-inch foam-plastic weather-stripping. You can get it in any hardware store; it comes with a sticky backing and compresses to practically no thickness. Once the strip was in place we turned the sheet over and drilled holes through the plexiglass and the weather-stripping. The holes drilled

The plexiglass windows are put into place with screws and washers. They fit flush with the frame, leaving a dead air space.

in the plexiglass were slightly larger than the screws to be used to secure it to the window frames. They were spaced six inches apart. While the storm window was held in place inside the RV, the window frame was drilled with the correct-size drill to take self-tapping metal screws. The weather-stripping insulated the bond between the two windows. Small washers were used under each screw to give the screw better support on the plexiglass.

In sub-zero weather the screw heads developed a film of frost, but our windows never frosted over.

This is not the ideal system, because our windows are now covered on the inside. We decided, therefore, to leave the window over the kitchen area as it was. It was small and the heat loss through it wouldn't be too great. That window could be opened for ventilation and the water that collected on it from condensation would run down into the sink, causing no damage.

We decided not to put a storm window on the windshield, either. It could have been done by using suction cups, but we found that we did well without it. The storm panes were removed when summer came, since our storm-window system did not provide for opening the windows.

HOT WATER . . . DON'T LET IT FREEZE

The hot-water tank presents a problem. Although it sits within the vehicle, it doesn't receive much warmth from the interior heat because of its own built-in insulation. By its very construction, one side of the heater is exposed to the outside. This presents a serious travel problem in the winter.

When you are parked, the gas will be lit whenever it's needed; it works fine. But while traveling it's very possible that the pilot flame may blow out. If this happened during a five-hour trip to a ski area, you could arrive there with a block of ice in the hot-water tank.

There are two answers to this problem. A shut-off valve can be installed on the water intake side of the tank. That way, the tank can be kept empty until you arrive at your destination. This will be inconvenient, but it'll do the job.

However, there is a better system—one that works like a charm. It's an optional feature called the Hot Water Motor Assist. Hot water from your driving engine is piped from the motor and connected to the coils in the hot-water tank. Thus the heat transfer system makes hot water as you drive along the highway. It's a good system for both summer and winter. In the summer it makes the engine run cooler; in the winter it keeps the tank from freezing while driving; and all year around you have hot water ready to gush out whenever you stop.

It is best to install this Hot Water Motor Assist when the unit is manufactured. To do it later is expensive.

There should be an easier way to light the hot water heater than to have to go outside in all kinds of weather to do the job. Try it on a cold windy night . . . in the rain or snow!

We bought two other items to take into sub-zero weather. One was a 1600-watt electric heater with its own blower. It's small, but it circulates a lot of air. We also took an infra-red lamp and holder, the common hardware store variety. You'll read soon how these proved to be well worth the investment.

In planning and thinking ahead for the new unit, Olive and I sat in the motor home in August with the air-conditioning on and tried to figure what our daily routine would be in January. She thought out such things as how to keep the rugs dry (a plastic mat to go over the rug near the door), how and where ski boots would be taken off, and where to string a line for wet clothes. I tried to figure out whether we might freeze up, and if so, how.

One result of this cogitation was that extra insulation was placed under the water pipes where they passed over the wheel wells. This is an area that has no insulation in most units. I traced all the water pipes and noted all areas where they had little protection from the weather. I wrapped and insulated these places with glass tape from the hardware store.

The whole unit was wired with No. 12 plus-ground electrical wire. Wall outlets were installed in areas where I thought I might have to place ordinary light bulbs for added warmth.

One outlet was placed in the bottom of a closet to hook up the battery charger, to get it out of the way; another was put so it was in a convenient place to work with an extension cord outside. When a wire had to be laid where it would cross the aisle or bathroom, I ran it under the floor, so the wire wouldn't show. Where these wires were exposed under the unit, I put them through a thin rubber hose. This was to protect them from abrasion by flying road stones.

The next problem was air circulation: since everything depended on a forced-air heating system, how could we be sure the air would circulate behind cupboards and cabinets and keep the pipes from freezing there? We cut holes in the sides of areas that presented a problem, because they covered pipes, and installed ten-inch louvers. We did the same thing in the backs of cabinets, so heat could reach the pipes that ran behind them. Louvers were placed in

117

the cabinet that held the water tanks. Whole areas were opened up, where the openings wouldn't be seen, in order to get air flow into cupboards. We tested the circulation in the middle of the summer with the air-conditioner. The temperature was taken inside the cabinets before the air-conditioner was put on. After it had run for an hour we took the temperatures again. The lower temperatures proved that air circulation was, in fact, taking place.

Stupidly, many manufacturers use a drain system for emptying the main water tanks that consists of dropping a four-inch pipe through the floor of the unit and putting a valve on the end of it. It would be just as easy for them to put the faucet valve inside the unit

The secret of keeping the pipes in the walls from freezing is air circulation. Louvered plates over cut-outs in the cabinet walls permit air flow.

and have only a drain pipe go through the floor. (Engineers please note . . . buyers, too.)

The first time I looked at this system was in mid-summer. I lay under my unit and cursed the guy who dreamed this one up. I guess he never thought that anyone would lie in the snow on a cold night and try to empty the tanks. The first thing needed—except for an inside valve—was a piece of garden hose so that when the valve under the floor was opened you could at least direct the deluge away from where you were lying. And how they ever expected anyone to open a second valve, for a second tank, while the water poured down from the first one is a good puzzle in engineering.

Arrows show flow of air. Cut-outs in cabinet walls allow air to pass into the vehicle wall containing the pipes, and into the next cabinet.

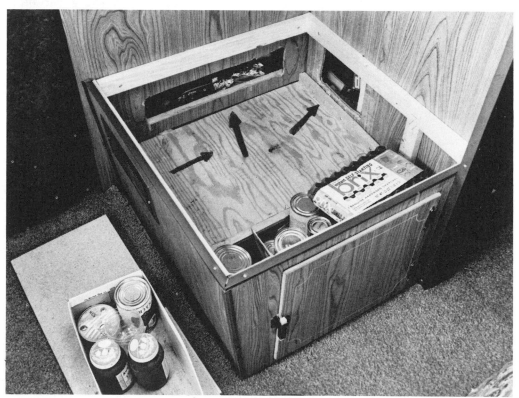

They should be able to do better than that for a guy who is spending more than $10,000 and who had always paid a boy to cut his grass!

As we readied our unit for winter, a big question was whether the pipe and valve below the unit would freeze in frigid weather. One engineer said no—the water inside would prevent it. Another engineer said yes. The solution was simple . . . electrical heating tape was put on the pipe and valve. Now either 110-volt outside current or the electric generator keeps the pipes and valves heated.

THE TEST . . . 20 BELOW

We've all lived in houses or apartments as long as we can remember. There are very few problems that arise around a house to which we don't know the answers. The comforts are the same in a motor home, but the thinking is different . . . you've got to think ahead. For example: although our trip north presented no driving problems, on first thought it seemed best, since there were two gasoline tanks on board, to use the one that was not connected to the gasoline-operated electric power generator. That way, if we did run into a problem and got stranded, we'd be sure to have 110-volt power. But then we realized that it wasn't wise to let the first tank go completely dry. One should switch to the second while one still has enough gas in the first to take one about fifty miles. It may be good to have electricity, but not at the cost of running dry.

Of course, the first thing you do on arriving at your destination is to fill all tanks. Think ahead.

When picking a place to park in ski country, face into the wind and try to park on the lee side of trees or some other formation that will give you some shelter from the wind. If you have to break into fresh snow to get settled, back into it. A motor home will go better forward in either mud or snow. You won't get stuck if you back into a questionable area; if the going gets tough, drive forward to get out.

In a motor home in cold weather, you have to live by rules. The door is for going in and out. Don't hold it open to talk. This also

120

holds true in the summer when you have the air-conditioning on.

Make an area where boots get put on and taken off, and don't wear them anywhere else in the unit. A plastic mat over the rug at that spot protects it. A coat hook near the door will be a big help. Wet things can be hung in the bathroom. Since winter clothes are bulky it's good to get them away into closets as soon as you can.

How much bottled gas is sixty pounds? In the summer it could take care of you for a month or more. Keep a record of how long the first bottle lasts in sub-zero weather. You'll find it will last about two or three days. This will vary. On one trip we almost had a serious problem. I had expected the bottled gas to last five days or more. At the end of two and a half days, I discovered the first bottle empty. A three-day weekend holiday was ahead of us and all the refill stations were closed. But the situation was easily solved. We turned the thermostat down to 55 degrees and used the supplementary electric heater to keep the temperature up to 70. The source of power was either our 110-volt hook-up or our on-board generator. It worked fine. Without that heater, though, we would have been in trouble.

The electric heater also pays off in other ways. Most of our windows, as I mentioned, are protected in the winter with storm panes. Those that are not protected freeze over from condensation. We may wake up in the mornings with an eighth of an inch of ice on them. Since we have electric outlets all over our motor home, it is easy to direct the heater onto the frozen windows. Then a few minutes with a sponge takes care of the problem.

We also use the electric heater to warm up the bathroom before a shower . . . it's better than at home. When the wind howls at night, we direct the heater to blow through the louvers into the fresh-water tank compartment. My wife has found other uses for the heater . . . it's the best hair drier she has ever had, and a fine boot-warmer.

POWER CONSERVATION

Our motor home is a traveling utility company, and in cold weather it is important to conserve our direct current from the batteries. While our automotive battery takes care of the engine needs for the vehicle, we have an extra heavy-duty battery for the household needs. Of course, we also have our gasoline-powered generator, which will produce 110-volt alternating current that can be converted to 12-volt DC. The generator uses about half a gallon of gasoline an hour. That means that with our forty-gallon tank we can generate electricity for eighty hours. Of course, if it's available, we have still one more source of electricity: with extension cords we can plug into outside 110-volt AC house current. Then we have no problem, since the house current will run the toaster, electric heaters, or any other household appliances we want to use. When converted to 12-volt DC, the 110 AC will also operate fans, blowers, and lights. By being plugged into this outside current we will use no electricity from the batteries; in fact, when we are plugged in, we keep a battery charger going to build the batteries up to capacity.

The real problem comes when we are parked in very cold weather and have to rely entirely upon our internal electrical supply. If we stay on battery the whole time we will run it down; and since the heating system depends on electrical current to turn the gas burners on and to run the blowers, it's important that we have juice. To conserve the batteries we alternate between using the generator and operating directly off the batteries. Here is how we do it.

When we get up in the morning the generator is started and the battery is built up with the charger, for the long night's work running the heater has taken a lot out of the battery. With the generator on we plug in the toaster and go about making breakfast. We even switch on a small, portable electric heater while the generator is running. We might as well use all the watts we are producing. The generator is kept on while we are doing our chores in the morning. When we leave to ski we turn it off and are now back on batteries. The thermostat is turned down to 60 and off we go. This will conserve gas and electricity. When we return in the evening we go back on the generator and get the battery built up for its long night's task. By running the generator a few hours morning and night we are able to stay ahead of the battery.

Every day or so we check the battery water with a hygrometer. Once in a while, the motor is started and the ammeter watched. If it shows a heavy charge and the needle falls within a few minutes, we know the battery is in good shape.

SEWAGE WATER . . . ANOTHER COLD-WEATHER PROBLEM

The holding tanks and drain pipes for sewage water are outside and underneath most motor homes. Whatever the outside temperature, they have to withstand it. This is not serious: a gallon of antifreeze will prevent any problem. Common table or rock salt will accomplish the same thing. Sink and shower water should be disposed of as soon as possible. A bucket with salt in it will keep the water from freezing. Recycling toilets are filled with an antifreeze recommended by the manufacturer.

Traps under sinks are no problem since they are inside the unit. However, they should not be forgotten when the motor home is not going to be used for a while. A half cup of antifreeze will keep them from causing any problem.

Still, on our first winter trip, I overlooked one thing. The trap under the floor of the shower, unlike the other traps, sits exposed to the outside. It froze solid!

INFRA-RED HEAT

With a frozen trap in our bathroom we had two choices to make. With glee, my daughter Gretchen suggested no more showers. For $10,000 worth of house, I decided on showers. The comedy of errors started. Boiling salt water was poured down the drain. The drain was too full of ice and the solution was useless. A skiing buddy suggested "dry gas." Now, how to get the salt water out to put the "dry gas" in? Use a straw, was the suggestion of the youngest member of the family, which renewed my faith in this new generation. Just when I was lying prone on the bathroom floor sucking brine out of the drain with a straw, some friends arrived for cocktails. There were two final results. One, the dry gas proved to be no better than the salt water. Two, one of the guests split his ski jacket laughing.

Up to that point the infra-red lamp had been completely forgotten. It was Olive who then came up with two excellent ideas that can be valuable on any such trip. First, she suggested using the heat lamp with an extension cord. When I told her it was too cold outside and the infra-red heat would dissipate too fast, she suggested making a tent out of aluminum cooking foil. The clamp on the bulb holder was to be fastened to the underside of the chassis. The lamp could be placed almost against the plastic pipe. By wrapping the holder, clamp, bulb, and frozen trap in the foil, the heat could do its job. A heat lamp must always be in a metal cage—it can scorch wood—and must never be left unattended. It all worked within five

In sub-zero weather an infra-red lamp will get you out of many a jam. Why didn't the manufacturers think to put a metal or Fiberglas shield over the valves to protect them from freezing road slush and mud?

minutes, but not before Olive came up with her second achievement of the day. How does one climb under a motor home with a few feet of snow on the ground? Simple, if you have a smart wife. First you move the vehicle and let the dual tires pack the snow down. Then you take a plastic tablecloth and spread it on the snow. You lie on the cloth and scoot around on your back as if you were on a sled. There, dear wife, credit where credit is due.

Later, acting on another suggestion by Olive, I tried using the commercial drain cleaner, Drāno. It creates a lot of heat and I found it, too, would thaw a frozen pipe. More credit to Olive.

I only wish some of the engineers deserved the credit, but instead they blunder over their drawing boards. We had to use the infra-red lamp again because the drain valves froze—not on the inside this time; antifreeze prevented that. The valves became covered with slush from the road. The slush turned to ice and built up until you couldn't even see the valves. A simple Fiberglas shield or a rubber mud-guard can prevent all of this. It also helps in the summer when the same valves become caked with mud.

TIPS FOR THE ENGINEERS

One of the problems of American industry is that designers and engineers are sometimes not sufficiently expert in their fields. So many of our products are made to look good, feel good, and be exquisitely packaged, but at the expense of their practical usefulness. A case in point: recently we bought our sixth American Motors car. They've been great or we wouldn't have repeated our purchases. With this year's model we received a new type of spare tire. It's collapsible and blows up with an aerosol can. It's a space-saver and so appealing that the manufacturers bought the idea.

Who made the decision to use these tires? That decision was made in the board room. It should have been made on the road in actual tryouts conducted by a test driver, then a whole family. Although we were skeptical of the idea in the first place, the auto salesman dispelled our fears—until one midnight when we were on the road on a holiday weekend. Loaded down with two kids, two dogs, and enough luggage to dress an army, we had a flat on a minor highway. The new-principle tire worked like a charm, at first. It looked like a collapsed tube sitting on the rim until the aerosol can was applied. In a jiffy it was full tire size. But then our problems started. The first was the flat tire. It was too big to be placed in the well where the collapsed tire had been stored. There was no room in the car for a dirty tire, plus four people and two eighty-pound dogs. With my pants belt, I finally tied the tire to the roof of the car. Then the next problem developed. The spare tire, so said the instructions—which our salesman had evidently never read—was good only for 2000 miles and speeds below 60 MPH. The book says the space-saver spare should not be driven over 200 miles for each installation. Obviously, this indicated that it was not a safe tire. The instructions advised us to drive to a gas station and have the original tire repaired. Try that at midnight on back roads on a holiday or Sunday night! Even at normal speeds we still had two hours' driving to do. At four in the morning, with both my spirits and my pants falling down, I decided to include this incident in this book in the hope that the men who sat in that American Motors board room making design decisions would read it.

In some ways, this kind of thinking is showing up in the recreation-vehicle industry. I earnestly suggest that company officials and engineers, with their families, take trips into sub-zero weather in their products. They will find that what they need for the winter will make a better product for the summer, too.

WHAT'S AHEAD FOR THE DESIGNERS?

The design engineers have two winter problems to face. One is simply to make the units livable in the bitter cold. A lot of people want to enjoy winter sports these days. I've shown you how we have gotten around some of these problems. But there is still another problem for those families who want to use their motor homes on winter weekends, a problem the industry doesn't seem to have recognized. There has been no provision for storing the vehicle for short periods of time without having the water system freeze up.

At this point in the construction of any unit, it would be so easy to wrap all the water pipes with electric heat tape. Then the skier could come home, plug the unit into the house current, and protect his water system.

What about the families who go away each weekend and then store the unit in their back yards from Sunday night to Friday evening? They have to go through a lot of work to protect their RVs, yet this recurrent nuisance could be avoided at very little extra cost at the time of manufacture, if only the designers would recognize the problem.

The procedure for emptying the fresh water out of an RV unit is rather time-consuming and difficult. Each manufacturer spells out the method for his unit. If it had to be done only once in the fall, the chore wouldn't be objectionable. But try doing it every Sunday night when you've finally reached home from a weekend of winter fun. You're tired and want to get to bed; but every drop of water has to be removed from the unit, or it'll freeze. Why not have a system whereby after driving home you could prevent freezing by plugging into your 110-volt house current? If the water pipes were wrapped with electrical heat tape when the unit was built, this could be done and there would be no problem. The fresh-water and hot-water tanks could be equipped with electric immersion heaters. They would only have to hold the water to 40 degrees or so.

127

IN SPITE OF IT, WINTER IS FUN IN AN RV

I've mentioned the problems involved in using your RV in winter weather and some of their solutions. When you know how to meet these problems, this is really the way to go! You don't get tied down to one winter sports place or one activity, and you have homelike comfort right at the site of the fun. Sitting in your little house with a snowstorm swirling around gives one a good feeling. Living this way involves you in the out-of-doors, and that's important in all seasons. It's a far cry from the way the prairie traveler lived, but you can be as close to nature as you want. That's what it's all about!

The outside temperature was 10 degrees below; with the wind chill factor it was minus 40 degrees. We were as snug as a bug in the rug my wife is hooking.

Tonight I sit in my warm study. The fire is going well; it has plenty of fuel. It was only last night that I sat in front of another fireplace all bundled up because someone hadn't planned for enough wood. I was on a winter cruise off Rhode Island with the publisher of *Motor Boating and Sailing* magazine and several of his staff. We were testing a new Fiberglas sloop. Why a shakedown cruise should be scheduled for November was beyond me, but I didn't have to be asked twice. The four of us aboard were experienced sailors. We knew what to wear, what to take, and how to pack. Except for enough coal for the mini-fireplace, I don't believe that in the three days aboard we found any other item we'd forgotten to bring. Yet on the second night out, while having a brandy to warm us, in place of the coal, we all agreed that we were badly organized below decks. It led to an interesting discussion on getting the most out of living in a confined area. Simple, everyday chores, if not done efficiently, get blown up out of proportion. Nerves start to rattle, and the fun goes up the funnel. For example, as experienced as we all were, we never found the dish towels until we emptied the boat at the end of the cruise. We all agreed that living in a confined area is an art . . . it takes more than a few brush strokes of planning and thinking.

As we sat reconsidering how we should have gone about stowing our gear, this story was told: It seems that a fellow was driving along a one-lane dirt road in the country and a big metal farm van pulled out in front of him. The road wasn't wide enough for the car to pass so the driver was forced to slow down to a crawl behind the truck. After two miles the truck stopped right in the middle of the road. The fellow behind, forced to stop, became exasperated, but then he saw a very strange thing happen. The farmer jumped out of the cab, reached behind the seat, and withdrew a baseball bat. He stepped quickly to the side of the truck, stopped, wound up with the bat, and whammed the metal side panel. Again he wound up and let one fly that could have sent a ball over the fence. Then he hurried back to the cab, replaced the bat, climbed up into the cab, and was off again, jolting along. The driver behind could do nothing but follow, shaking his head. Two miles later the same thing happened again. The truck stopped, the driver clambered down, bat in hand, slugged the panel twice, got back in the cab, and off again.

Every two miles, for twenty miles, the same thing occurred. The truck was whopped. The attitude of the driver behind turned from frustration to absolute fascination with this unexplained behavior. At a gas station, the road finally opened up. The truck went in for fuel. The car could now go on, but it didn't. The driver's curiosity had gotten the better of him, and he turned into the station. While they were both getting gas the driver asked the farmer what that strange business was all about.

"Well, you see, mister," said the farmer, "I got me a five-ton truck here. I'm carrying ten tons of chickens. I have to whup the truck a good crack to keep half them critters flying."

There's a moral to this story for sailors of the sea or of the land. To stow things efficiently and avoid wasting space, get things in the air. Hang them up. Don't use up the valuable floor space, use the air above it. Here are some applications of this principle that we've found especially helpful.

SHOES . . . WHEN NOT ON THE FEET

Boots, sneakers, dress shoes, slippers, ski boots, and other footwear can turn you into a traveling shoe store if you're not careful. Multiply the list by the number in your party and you could make a shoemaker happy.

Convince the little woman to use restraint: one pair of dress shoes, smartly selected, should do the job. Rubber camp boots for all are a good investment. The best we have found are the L. L. Bean type—rubber bottoms, leather tops with no laces. The rest of the footwear is dealer's choice, depending on your thing and the season.

There are a number of ways to carry shoes. You can buy a shoe bag that hangs on a clothes rod. These work fine except that they take up too much space in the closet. Since a closet has four walls, a

Every available space must be used, but keep the floor free.
Shoe bags prevent a mess—and they are easy to make.

floor and a ceiling, plus the space in between, we might as well use it all. We solved the shoe problem on my wife's sewing machine. We found the best place for shoes was to hang them in home-sewn bags on the doors of the closets. Open the door and there they are, ready to be put on. Since this is also a good place for the long mirror, a must for a woman, the shoe bags were designed to fit all around it.

Certain cabinet doors can be completely lined with shoe bags. Boots are another matter. They'll be too heavy and will have to be put on the floor of the closet. If the closet is very deep there is no reason not to build a shelf in the rear so the boots can be stored on different levels. In one unit we even put a light near the floor so we could see what we were getting.

Two or three pairs of ski boots can really cause a space problem. Like the chickens, you have to put them in the air. Ski boots should be stored in their carriers, to preserve their shape and make them easier to carry. String them from the top to the bottom of the closet, one above the other on 3/8-inch shock cord. A hook at the top and bottom will hold them in place. Short pieces of rubber shock cord with hooks at each end, attached between the boot holders, make up the string.

Shoe bags have other uses besides storing shoes. They can hold all sorts of items. We've seen them used for maps, gloves, wool hats, and even keys. The inside of any cupboard door that otherwise would not be used makes a fine place to hang a bag. A shoe bag hung next to the driver's chair in a motor home makes a good place to store cigarettes, gum, matches, sunglasses, and other personal belongings.

CHAIRS . . . WHAT TO DO WITH THEM WHEN YOU DON'T SIT IN 'EM

Beach chairs or folding chairs or whatever you want to call them have caused more grief in our travels than I care to recall. Where do you put them? We've strapped them on the back of the RV. They got so filthy we couldn't use them. We tried the top; that was a little better. They were cleaner but harder to get at. Then we de-

Folding chairs are always a problem. Hanging them gets them out of the way. We did it with cloth straps. Note, reflected in the mirror, the two hanging bags. They contain our rain gear.

cided to make a protective bag for them. The bag became a mess to work with. I finally left the damn chairs home. Need I say that plan didn't go over so well? I had to agree. Sitting on a makeshift arrangement to enjoy the last part of the day with drink in hand isn't what I'd call living in style.

The solution we finally found was an easy one. But I'd spent a lot of money to get there. We had bought all kinds of chairs over the years. It wasn't until we found, at a supermarket, a metal frame chair that folded completely flat that the problem was solved.

Now we had something with which we could apply the chicken theory. Cloth straps and boat snaps were used to hang the chairs on the inside of a closet wall, one above the other. They take up only one inch of space and are left there summer and winter. They're never in the way and they're easy to get at when we need them. We were careful to hang them so they fit snugly against the wall. Rattling chairs can be as much of a problem for the nerves as ones you have to struggle to get at.

133

RAIN, RAIN . . . GO AWAY

The best way to get rain is to forget the rain gear. We have our gear on board year round, and it doesn't take up space hanging in the closet. We use the very thin rubberized nylon jacket and pants sets. Each member of the family has his own. Simple bags were made with a draw string. Each bag was marked with the initial of the owner . . . or differently colored bags can be made. They hang above one another in the corner of the closet. A bag about the size of a quart of milk will do the job, because these jacket and pants sets roll up to practically nothing.

When someone comes in with a wet rain suit on, he takes it off at the door. It's then hung in the bathroom to dry. Once dry, it's rolled up, put in the bag and out of sight.

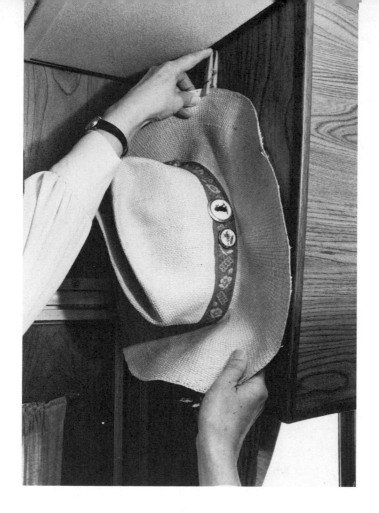

HATS . . . WHERE DO THEY GO IF NOT ON THE HEAD?

Women's big-brimmed hats are a problem. Someone is always sitting on them . . . but the answer to this is easy. At the top of the wall, over the door, we secure a couple of colored clothes pins. We use a color that goes well with the decor. One side of each pin is drilled to take a screw and it's placed on the wall at the ceiling. When you want to hang the hat up, push on a pin and stick the brim in. The hat is up, out of the way, and it will stay there.

We have these pins near the door because that's the place you'll be when you want to grab your hat. We also have a couple in the top of a closet for storage. It's otherwise wasted space, and it keeps the hats out of sight.

Space savers . . . three pairs of pants on one hanger, plus a coat.

CLOTHES HANGERS

Boat supply outlets sell a clothes hanger that makes a lot of sense for small closets. A coat can be hung on the hanger in the normal way, but it's built so that three pairs of pants can be hung on the bars below. It really saves space, and the pants are held in place so they won't slip off while traveling.

Women sometimes have a problem keeping a dress on its hanger, especially if it's one of those shoulder-strap affairs. Take two rubber bands and wind one on each end of a simple wooden hanger. The strap can't slip off. Skirts can be pinned on a wire hanger.

DIRTY CLOTHES . . . A HEADACHE

My complaint that manufacturers think more about RV units sitting in a showroom than in a campsite holds true when it comes to dirty clothes. I've seen only one unit that made provision for a built-in laundry hamper. So we've solved the dirty clothes problem another way. Again, we hang the laundry bags—in this case they're hung from the coat rack in the closet. We have designed the two bags so they hang about sixteen inches above the floor. Their tops are attached to cloth supports suspended from a heavy wooden

136

Dirty laundry is a problem. We have solved it by hanging two bags on a coat hanger. The dark bag holds dark clothes; the other is for light-colored clothes. The left picture shows how far we drop the bags from the bar of the hanger so the bags will not take up coat space on the rack. Unbutton the bags when full, and the clothes are ready for washing . . . no sorting.

hanger. When they get full they are below the valuable clothes hanging space. Both bags hang completely open at the top. That makes it easy to put in the soiled clothes. There's a dark bag for dark clothes; a light one for light clothes. The bags are attached to the straps with buttons. When the clothes are to be taken to the laundromat the bags are unbuttoned and closed with a draw string at the top.

137

The rule is to hang things. The waste-paper basket is hooked to the wall with a wire coat-hanger bracket that we made in five minutes. Even pans with a lip can be hung; they fit into wooden brackets you can make in ten minutes.

WASTE—PAPER AND GARBAGE

If there is any group that is more conscious of our ecology than the RVers it would be hard to find. The world is their oyster, and by-and-large they seem good about protecting it. Of course there are always some slobs around. A fellow traveler told me this story: he and his family had found a grand spot with a sensational view. They got the chairs out to sit and look for a spell. When they settled themselves they noticed something was wrong. Without saying a word to each other, they simultaneously got up, spent twenty minutes cleaning up the trash others had left . . . then they got back to enjoying the spot.

There are two main areas in a motor home that present the trash problem. In the driving area we carry two small trash baskets, one for each chair. We made them in fifteen minutes, and they cost practically nothing. We bought six-inch-square plastic refrigerator containers. We cut a round hole in each lid with a pen knife. For a base we used a scrap of rubber floor-mat ten inches or so long and six inches wide. We put small nuts through the mat and the bottom of the box and fastened them with nuts inside. The attached mat on the base prevents the box from falling over. Set this on the floor at your fingertips and you have a simple, handy trash dispose-all.

The trash problem in the living area is somewhat bigger. Of course everyone uses plastic bags as liners in the trash basket. The question is where to put the basket so it'll be out of sight and won't turn over. Back to the chickens . . . we hang the basket on the inside of a low cabinet door. Buy a square plastic basket with a strong lip around the top. They come in all sizes at hardware stores. Make sure the basket isn't as tall as the door. Attach it to the door with coat-hanger wire. A pair of pliers and a vice are the only tools you'll need. Cut the coat hanger and straighten it out. Put a small loop in one end. Then bend the hanger wire so it fits snugly under the lip of the basket. You'll only have to go around three sides of the basket. Cut the wire off and make a small loop at that end. Bend the loops so they will be against the door. Make the loops small. Put a washer over each loop and a screw through the washer and into the door; now the wire loops will be secured to the door. The basket slips down into the wire holder. The lip prevents the basket from falling through or tipping. Line it with a plastic bag. The basket swings out automatically. Open the door when you want to use it; close the door and it's all out of sight. If you keep the basket near the top of the door, you still have available floor space underneath it.

Up in the driving area we have trash baskets made from plastic refrigerator containers. Cut a hole in the top and bolt the container to a rubber mat base so it won't tip over while driving.

Cans, bottles, and all the things you have to carry to keep things clean always seem to fall over . . . after they've been opened. The solution to this problem is two strands of 3/8-inch elastic shock cord. Stretch the shock cord and hook it on the wall inside a cabinet near the floor. One piece should be about three inches off the floor and the other about six inches. Slip boxes and bottles between the cord and the wall. The cord will hold them in place.

To carry soap flakes or the large bulk soaps, pack them in heavy plastic bags before you start out. Then as you use them you actually gain space. This same technique should be used for dry cereals and dog food.

In one camper we had, we found the perfect place to store items that were not used every day. We discovered space down on the floor, under a drawer, going to waste. We have to pull out the drawer to get at the things we've stored underneath it, but if they are not going to be used that often it really doesn't matter.

Storage space and the way you use it is really the secret to happy living on wheels. Let's assume that you have selected a unit with enough cabinets around the ceiling. Check when buying: some makers offer extra cabinets optionally. Take them; you'll use them. A problem with most units, however, is that they don't provide any shelving in the cabinets. Some units will have a shelf in the cabinet over the cooking area but not in any others. As a result, only about half of the space in the cabinets is useful. You can't pile clothes high enough to fill the available space. See if you can have shelves installed when you order a unit. If not, you'll have to do it yourself. It's not an easy job putting a shelf in a cabinet that is already assembled. It should be done when the cabinet is put together.

In most units there is a storage area on the floor over the wheel housing. It's rounded and represents a poor use of space. Put a board over it, secure it to the walls, and make it into a shelf.

This cabinet was built over a wheel well. The curve of the fender-shaped wheel cover made the space useless for storage. When covered over with a piece of plywood, it became a good shelf for storing canned goods.

STORAGE UNDER THE SEATS

One would assume that there is a good amount of space under divans and seats in an RV unit. But with all the appliances—water heaters, space heaters, water tanks, bottled gas, generators—there is little space left. Therefore every inch of unused space should be considered for storage purposes.

If some of the appliances do not take up the full height of the space under a seat or bed, a false floor should be put in so the extra space can be used for storing other articles. It may be only a few inches, but you'll be glad for it. We have made one such otherwise wasted space into a place to store tow chains, winches, shovels, and other such items that aren't used often but must be carried.

A useless area turned into storage space.

A tip: if you have a gas heater under one of the beds, cover it with either insulation board or asbestos; otherwise the person in the bed gets too warm.

Getting into these box storage spaces under the beds is usually a difficult chore for a woman. First the pillows and cushions have to be removed, then the lid to the storage space must be lifted and removed. That's not easy if it's a six-foot bed. We've simplified the job by cutting the lids into manageable sizes, two- or three-foot

142

lengths. Then we drill 1½-inch holes into the lids so a finger can be put through the board to make lifting easy. You may have to put extra supports across the space so the cut lid won't sag when sat upon. You will find that loading such a compartment is easier from the top than through the door on the side.

We have even used this wrinkle in an area no bigger than one seat. The board was cut in half and thumb holes were put in. Now we can get to the back of that space by tilting the cushion up and taking out only a half section of board. It's a time-saver. .

Manufacturers spend as little time as possible on the insides of all spaces. Units all look good with the doors closed . . . they leave the inside spaces for you to figure out.

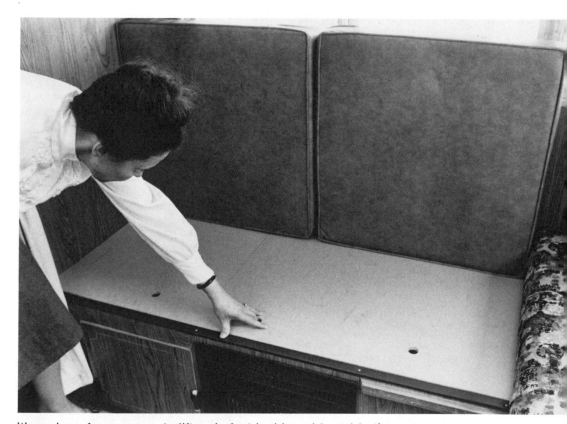

It's a chore for a woman to lift a six-foot bed board to get to the space below. Turn the page and see how we easily solved this problem.

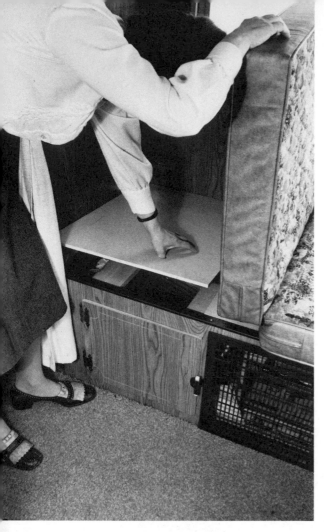

By simply dividing the long board we made the job easy. New thumb holes were drilled, supports added under the cuts to keep seat from sagging.

We even divided the lids of the small seats. That way, we found it was easier to reach items toward the rear of the cabinet. We open the door only for things in the front area.

144

WHERE TO STORE . . . AND HOW

The joke around our house, when we're set to go in the motor home, is—where is the piano? Someone always comes up with some sort of a smart-alec answer.

In such a small area, everything has to have its place. Pots and pans that fit into each other go into one low cupboard. Canned and bottled goods go into another low cabinet. Canned goods and heavy items should be stored on the floor or as low as possible. Light things go above.

We've found that in addition to the things that hang in the closet, other clothes should also be handled differently from at home. Each member of the family is given two or more cabinets around the ceiling. We pack everything in clear plastic shoe and sweater boxes. Each person's socks and ties and such go into one box. Underwear goes in another. Shirts are put in the sweater-size box. Then all other items are packed around on the shelves. It makes life a little easier for a guy like me who can lose a necktie unless he has it on. Things don't get messed up while you're scrounging around looking.

Dividing shelves is a must, and plastic boxes keep things organized.

Food, except for canned goods, is handled the same way. We've collected plastic boxes of all sizes for the hundred-and-one things the cook has above the sink. It's easier to pull out one box that contains all the seasonings than it is to find a special seasoning somewhere on a shelf above your head. It's important, too, that the shelf be well organized and that things go back where they came from after they're used.

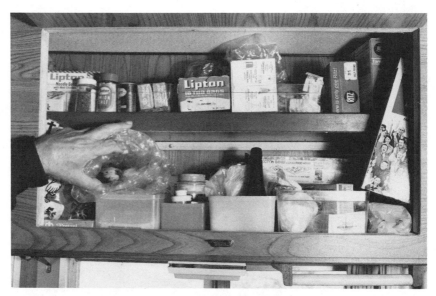

Foodstuffs should be placed in plastic containers; otherwise they'll be all jumbled together when you arrive at the campsite.

Every woman knows how to store the silverware and utensils in a kitchen drawer. You can either buy dividers in a hardware store or make them out of boxes. When it comes to the medicine cabinet . . . that's another story. Most people don't do a good job even in their own homes. A medicine cabinet with a light is a good optional feature to have in an RV, especially for Daddy. It's always fine for shaving, but don't open it unless it's properly organized. Everything

146

that goes in the medicine cabinet must go in small boxes the depth of the shelves. It's a simple matter then to organize the contents, and if this system is used things won't slide all over while traveling. You can even label the boxes if you want to be that fussy.

Packing the refrigerator is much the same as packing the medicine cabinet. In both cases, items are grouped together in a logical way.

Medicines and similar items should also be stored in plastic boxes. That not only keeps them from falling out when the medicine cabinet is opened, but makes it easy to find things fast.

DISHES AND THINGS

Sailors really get the credit for best solving the problems of storage of dishes, cups, and so forth, but there are a few twists that they can learn too. There was a time when you went camping with a metal plate and a cup and were happy if the coffee was hot and the food plentiful. Modern plastics and packaging have changed all that. Today we have plastic dishes for the main meal and plastic-coated paper for minor eating events. The same goes for drinking utensils. Storage of all these items becomes a problem.

As far as the dishes are concerned, a rack to fit the different-sized plates can be either bought or made. It keeps the dishes from scattering all over the cabinet when we stop at a red light. The cups and saucers are handled in the same way. The cups sit on top of one another. They slip into a holder and can be lifted out easily by the handles.

We have these holders attached to the wall of a top cabinet for quick access. We stack plastic glasses one inside the other, and then elastic tape—the kind that used to be used in garters—is stretched around the bottom glass and attached to the wall. They'll all stand securely in little space.

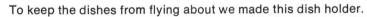

To keep the dishes from flying about we made this dish holder.

Cups are easy to get out of this container. Just put a finger through the handle and lift. The plastic glasses are stacked and held in place with elastic. Bowls are a problem. If only they could substitute as hats!

Stacks of paper plates of all sizes are held on the inside of the cabinet door with home-made elastic holders. This was my wife's brilliant idea.

Paper-dish storage is a real fun thing. The picture shows a holder for the inside of a door. You'll have to make one yourself. You'll need a few yards of elastic and a simple grommet maker. Any sewing counter sells this item. The grommets hold the tape together and through them you can also screw the whole thing to the inside of a door. The picture shows how it works. The tape will stretch to hold two packages of paper plates of different sizes. As the supply diminishes the elastic holds the remaining plates securely. The plates are at your fingertips. It's the chickens-in-the-air theory again.

Even platters come in plastic-coated paper. They take up a lot of space and usually have to go on the bottom of everything else. Not so with the elastic hangers. Put them inside a cabinet, on the ceiling. The elastic tape, attached by screws through the grommets, will make them accessible.

Paper cups are a must to free the cook of washing. A paper-cup dispenser should be mounted near the sink. You can buy one in any

150

store. We covered our store-bought variety with scraps of wood that we asked the RV manufacturer to send to us. It's just a simple wooden box, but it fits in with the rest of the paneling. It doesn't do the job any better, but you'd be surprised how many people notice it. If you're going to have the chickens in the air, you might as well have them look like pheasant.

Paper napkins can be handled in the same way as the plates. You can buy a holder that takes about fifty napkins. It can be screwed to the inside of a cabinet door, and a piece of elastic can be put around it from side to side to prevent the napkins from falling out.

Some day I'll have to think of a way to handle big salad bowls. They are always in the way . . . maybe they could be designed to double as hats.

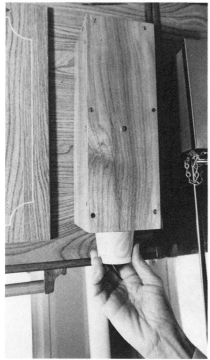

Little things: Scraps of matching wood were used to make this paper cup holder. Paper clip keeps towels from unraveling while en route.

Daytime storage of bedding is a real problem. We've solved it by

BEDDING . . . WHERE DOES IT GO DURING THE DAY?

Once while we were traveling through the Midwest we met an interesting family. Somehow we got talking about motor homes—a better way to make friends than talking about the weather or borrowing a cup of sugar. Before we knew it, they were showing us the interior of their brand-new second home. We got together for a drink later to continue our discussion. The woman of the family looked more like the type who would be happier sitting on the Riviera than traveling in an RV. As we sat around talking equipment, she finally made a confession. There was one part of this new

aking night covers our daytime cushions. It eliminates storing.

life she didn't like—making up all the beds in the evening and undoing them the next day. The worst part was folding all the sheets and covers and stowing them in the cabinet under the bunk. We assured her that we could solve her problem with ease. My wife gave her a first-hand demonstration.

Sheets, blankets, and pillows take up a lot of storage space in the daytime, and are truly a pain in the neck for the wife to handle. We've come upon a whole new system. First, we dispense with sheets. Instead we use Acrilan blankets. Some call them boat blankets. They are very soft and go through the washing machine without any problem. We cut a foot or so off the bottom of the

Here is our bedding during the daytime.

blanket, fold it in two, and sew a zipper up the side and across the foot. This makes the blanket into a light-weight sleeping bag. It's fine for sleeping and no problem to make up in a bed. Then comes the best part . . . in the daytime we use these sleeping bags as cushions. We fold them up and put them into cloth cases which are really cushion covers. They look great and add a lot of comfort to the lounge. I guess if someone insisted, sheets could be folded up and stored in the cushion covers too, but these blankets are so comfortable that the most fastidious sleeper would enjoy them without a sheet.

If the wife isn't good with a sewing machine, trade her in for a new one or have the local slipcover people make the bags for a few dollars. The sleeping pillows are handled in the same way. Each goes into a gaily colored bag that zips closed during the day.

Our new friend was so pleased with this idea that we have been receiving Christmas cards from her ever since. It's strange that this idea has not been made into a commercial item. So few RVers know about it; boat people have been doing it for years.

154

One of the first things most wives notice in the RV showroom are the "cute little curtains." This is where most manufacturers go to town putting together good color combinations. The larger companies hire decorators to pick fabrics and plan the decor. They can make a unit look good on the display floor, but that doesn't mean it's practical for the road. If the prime purpose is color and color alone, they are successful, but they'd do better if they got out on the turnpikes and learned the problems you encounter there.

For one thing, many of the curtain fabrics selected are too light in color and too thin. Often in campsites or other parking places there are floodlights on all night. Delicate, light-colored materials will not darken the interior of a motor home enough for sleeping. Even a bright moonlight night can create a problem. Temporarily, this can be solved by hanging beach towels over the rods and in effect making a lining for the curtains.

The time is 6 A.M. Who could sleep in such bright light without covering his head? Whoever picked the curtain material considered showroom appeal, but not practicality. Photo on next page shows better thinking.

Light-proof shades darken the sleeping area even during the day.

If you have a choice of curtain material when ordering a unit, however, pick something that will solve this problem. We've never been successful on this score and have always ended up making our own. It seems a shame to spend the money for curtains that come with the vehicle and then have to go to the expense of new fabric, plus the time it takes to run them up on a sewing machine, but that's the way it is. If you are going to make your own curtains, use a heavy, opaque material or better yet, plan to make them of two thicknesses. The outside material should be heavy enough to keep out the light and the inside should be bright in color to give an airy feeling to the interior when the curtains are closed. Dark colors on the interior give one a closed-in feeling in a small area.

Another problem is that some RV manufacturers are using the wrong hardware. Drive down the road with metal curtain rings strung on a metal rod and it'll sound like a Melanesian court dancer doing a bracelet dance. Try that for three hundred miles a day. The only thing you can do about it is to replace the metal rings with nylon or cloth ones.

There is another complaint on the curtain score . . . why do some makers use materials that have to be dry cleaned or pressed? It would be such a help to be able to put them in a washing machine. With all the dusty traveling, these curtains take more punishment than the ones at home.

156

MORE CURTAIN TIPS

For divided curtains, install decorative snaps on the edges that meet in the center, so when you close them, they'll stay that way.

Some units do not have interior curtains to divide the living spaces. It's a very simple matter to mount a flush track on the ceiling and make a curtain to run on it. It'll not only give dressing and sleeping privacy, but you'll find that after a night's sleep with the windows open in the bedroom area, the curtains will keep the rest of the motor home warm.

CURTAINS . . . MORE THAN JUST PRIVACY

Most motor homes have a ceiling track for a long curtain to be drawn across while driving at night, and it's very useful for the driver. With it drawn, the interior lights behind him will not reflect in the windshield. This curtain is also useful in cold country. The large expanse of windshield glass transmits a lot of cold air. With this curtain drawn you have that much less area to heat when you are parked. A short curtain on this same track makes a fine storage area out of the front bunk . . . there's plenty of room in there and the curtain hides all the junk. When Olive and I are traveling without the kids, we get everything up there except the piano. When not in use, this small curtain is stored against the opposite wall from the driver's curtain; either one can then be used on the same track without interference.

A tip: the curtain over the sink area can get splashed with water or food. A clear plastic curtain inside the regular one will protect it.

Two curtains on the one track solve two problems. The long night-driving curtain can be used both winter and summer as insulation from the windshield glass. The small upper curtain covers the bunk area.

If you have a screen door you'll most likely have a problem closing the curtain on the outside door at night. The pictures show what the problem is. The screen door must be opened, the two doors separated, the curtain closed, the screen door latched back to the main door, and the whole thing closed. This operation has to be done with you standing outside. Try that on a cold, rainy night or anytime it's below zero. There is a simple way around it. A small curtain on two boat snaps will do the trick. The curtain is put up and taken down from the inside. The snaps are screwed in above the door frame and the curtain hangs down over the window. You've got privacy without getting wet.

Whoever designed the curtains on this door never had to use them on a stormy night! To close them, one has to go outside (*top left*), open the screen door, close the curtains, close the screen door and then close both doors. How much simpler it is to do it our way—snap on a curtain indoors.

If your RV has a tailgate, it can give you a whole new living area, with the aid of a curtain. All kinds of tools and equipment can be stored in the rear compartment, and when the tailgate door swings down it makes a good workshop table. A colorful plastic curtain to cover the open compartment and all its junk makes the open tailgate a good-looking place for an outside bar and serving area. The plastic should be long enough not only to cover the tools and equipment but also to fold over and act as a tablecloth. Set the hibachi on it, put out the plates, and you have a fine patio.

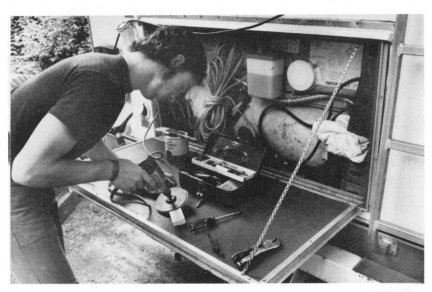

Gimbal holders for drinks can prevent accidents . . . pipe holders are good, too.

USEFUL GADGETS . . . AND SOME TIPS

RVers seem to be gadgeteers; it goes with the breed. The recreation magazines are full of ads for all sorts of ingenious creations from awnings to Lazy Susans. It will be hard to tell you exactly which things in this line will be good for you and your particular unit. All I can do is mention those items that we have found successful and let you go on from there.

GIMBALS

Two holders for drinking glasses, hung on gimbals in the cockpit area, are a real treat. A drink of hot coffee while driving is very refreshing but normally difficult to handle. The gimballed holder, which can be bought in any boat-supply store, makes it easy going. With one of these, we don't have to stop for our coffee break. Extra coffee is brewed at breakfast time and stored in a thermos until coffee time. The thermos eliminates the need to light the stove while underway. We also use thermos-type, plastic glasses to hold the hot drink so it won't burn our fingers. We even found a couple of these glasses to match our wood interior. Sloshing, as you drive, can cause a problem, but we get around that by using large glasses, not too full, and drinking through a straw. A gimballed holder on the wall next to each chair makes coffee time fun and not a disaster.

161

ASH TRAYS

The boating fraternity have been at this game longer than we have, so they've come up with some other choice items. For the smoker, they have an ash tray that won't tip or slide. It has a sand- or shot-filled pouch as a base. We always have one on the dash. For the pipe smoker, who is always laying down his pipe and making a mess, there is a simple rack that holds the pipe upright. In our lounge area we have two ash trays mounted on the wall in holders. Each ash tray can be lifted out and a glass can be slipped down into its holder instead. Although they don't swivel like real gimbals, these holders will prevent a glass from tipping over while underway.

HAND-HOLDS

I have found handrails very important on the road. Like seat belts, they're a good safety device. We have one grab rail in the cooking area. Such rails are easy enough to make yourself, or you can buy them at a hardware or boat store. If they're made of wood they'll blend in with the rest of the interior. They have saved my wife many a bump. Often while I'm driving she'll prepare a snack, and right in the middle of things she'll have to grab on. It works well; she's still around.

A hand grasp at the entrance is also a good idea. I don't know why manufacturers do not change their system and build in doors much like those in many buses. When the bus door opens the step

162

Grab handles make life easier and safer.

goes down automatically; it comes up when the door closes. The RVs have a step that has to be put up and down by hand. That means that the first person out has to make a giant stride to reach the ground. Then he has to bend over and pull out the step. This giant step is a real problem for old folks and kids, getting in as well as out. We've installed a hand grasp at the door so a person may pull himself up if need be. It's also a big help if the last one in is carrying a package.

One more gimmick in this field. Over the ignition switch we have a small sign that reads, "Is the step up . . . Stupid?" If a side-door step is left protruding while you're moving, it could raise havoc with fire plugs . . . and dogs wouldn't like that.

PILOT LIGHTER

A good gadget for lighting all gas appliances is the butane cigarette or pipe lighter previously mentioned in connection with the stove. It's especially helpful for an appliance that must be lit on the outside of the unit. Just try to light a water heater in a brisk wind with wooden matches. Keep the kids away . . . because of your language. The flame must heat the element long enough to open the gas flow. Before we finally bought the butane lighter with the adjustable flame size, we tried to light these utilities using the "blanket method." When it was windy my wife held a blanket around me and against the wall. I'd work inside this contraption trying to light the hot water heater. Sorry I never got a picture of that.

EXTINGUISHERS

We carry two fire extinguishers. One is inside, near the rear of the coach, and the other is near the door. They have to be easy to get. I've used one only once but I was thankful that it was in easy reach and fully charged. Twice a year they should be checked. The CO_2 type is best and is available at automotive stores.

TIPS

Now for some less exciting tips. Most units come through with only one towel rack in the bathroom. We've taken one wall in the compartment and put in racks almost from floor to ceiling. Dish towels hang there, out of sight, to dry. We have a rack for the floor mat that we use just outside the shower. Everybody has his own place for his towels. It's simple, and it helps make life easy.

You might think that clothes hooks need no particular discussion. Not so. My advice here is, don't move too fast. Any time we've started outfitting a new RV we wait many weeks before installing the hooks. You'll find that as you learn to live in the space, certain procedures will develop. Simple things, such as

164

undressing for bed, will be done differently in a motor home than at home. Do it a number of times, then put the hooks up. Of course, inside closets it's a slightly different matter. If you want to change the hooks there later, the screw holes won't show. Think out the clothes-hanging problem for dressing, for sleeping, and for out-doors. Maybe you'll need a few extra hooks at the door for guests who come in wet. Think it all out, if possible getting into other RV units and seeing their tricks.

The engineers have a name for this: time and motion study. No matter what you are going to hang or install, make sure you work it all out, run through the job, and then drill the holes. I guess I learned the hard way. In my first unit, if Olive was already in bed, I had to climb over her to hang up the shirt I'd taken off. That was surely changed fast.

SMALL TIPS

Most women know all the gadgets needed for cooking, but there is another item in the commissary department that might be over-looked . . . ice cubes. You may need an extra tray or two. We have also found that a portable bar is a good item. Some folks build a container for bottles in a cabinet. We use a home-made box with separators for the bottles. We can carry the whole thing outdoors or set it on the table in the lounge area.

Nothing like a portable bar made from a wooden wine shipping case!

An inside-outside thermometer is another good thing to have. We do it the inexpensive way, a dollar thermometer glued to the wall inside, and one outside the window.

We've talked about the electric heater. Ours is 1650 watts. The important thing about an electric heater is the fan; ours moves 350 cubic feet a minute. The whole thing measures eight by nine by five inches and weighs only six pounds. It's made by the Electric Trading Company in New York City. Most electric fans are used by placing them on the floor, where the air is the coolest. This heater makes such a strong flow of air that the company recommends placing it near the ceiling and pointing it down. It picks up the hot air at the ceiling and directs it back down toward the floor. The five-inch turbine really pushes out the air.

Another small tip: you should check with your motor-home dealer and get a list of extra parts to carry with you. Fan belts of each size you require are a must. I've spent two days in the back country trying to find one. Extra fuses and bulbs should also be on the list.

We have one dollar thermometer inside and another glued to the outside of one window, so we can read it from the inside.

STEAL-PROOF

There are a lot of stories around about motor homes and campers being stolen. It's been suggested that it has to be done by an organized ring of thieves. Whether the vehicles are being shipped out of the country or to remote places isn't really known. One dealer lost three in one year, and plenty of individuals have lost them too. I hate to tell you how to protect yourself against this, because it gives away my secret. Crooks know all the tricks involving jumping switches in the electrical system. Of course you could carry the distributor in your pocket. My way is cleaner. I've cut the gas line. I had a "T" inserted in the line and a tube run into the inside of a cabinet in the motor home. A shut-off valve was connected to the end of the line, inside the cabinet. When I park, the valve is opened. If the engine is started, it'll burn the gasoline that's in the carburetor and then conk out because the fuel pump will suck in air, not gasoline. A crook now has a vehicle that has moved about fifty feet. Even if he should guess the reason, it'd take a lot of time to trace out the problem and find the valve. With the valve closed the engine operates normally.

P.S. Remember to close it before you start up.

167

From scraps of wood that match the interior paneling, we built this cabinet in the wasted space beside the door.

WOODEN THINGS

When you place the order for your RV, ask the dealer to include scraps of the interior paneling and a few sets of matching hinges and door pulls. I've seen these units being made and the scraps that get thrown away would make a carpenter sick. You may find that a small shelf or bookcase would be good to have. There's very little waste space in most of the units today, but what little there is can be made very useful. For example, we found some wasted space under the co-pilot's seat, near the door, and it's necessary to store all sorts of things near the door. A matching cabinet there looks great and saves many a step, since it can be reached from the outside as well as from within. Two things we keep there are a truck-tire gauge for testing the inside tire on duals and a trucker's bat for testing all the tires by their sound.

This is just one example. Get the scraps and you'll find plenty of uses for them, even if it's just a simple cutting board for the wife. In the case of the tire gauge and bat, I'm sure I wouldn't test the tires as often as I do if implements for it weren't right at my fingertips. After all, gadgets are to help simplify things and cut down on problems.

In one of our early campers we built boxes for storage under the floor. Access doors were cut into the skirt of the camper. These boxes—we nicknamed them "the wine cellars"—gave us a lot of extra storage space. For our latest RV (*below*), we ordered extra "cellars." We found space to install two of them. They're good for storing dirty items.

Citizens' band radio can be a very useful addition to recreation living. It's a good way to stay in touch while rolling or parked. My first thought about CB radio was to stay as far away from it as possible. It's just a substitute for a telephone, and who needs that when you're trying to get away from phones, TV, and such on vacation. It was Olive who convinced me that it was a necessity.

On our first trip deep into the back country of Canada we found the two-way radio very reassuring as well as useful. Since we were fishing there alone, Olive wanted a means of contacting the outside world in case of emergency. No emergency arose, but we did get some help from a Mr. Bates, whom we never met. We enjoyed talking to him on CB every few nights, and when we started to run low on LP gas he saved us a lot of time by telling us where we could find it. His opening remark each time we spoke to him was, "How's the fishing, and are you folks all right?" City folks would be surprised how much the country people depend on citizens' band radio for their communications. It's a working tool for them and they appreciate it when other users don't just gab on it as if it were a telephone.

CB can also be used to put through long-distance phone calls. We have done this often; when important information was needed we'd call and ask for someone who had a telephone to answer us. Our radio radius is about thirty-five miles. We would ask them to make a reverse-charge call to our party, tell them what to say and what answer we expected. When the call was completed we'd get our answers back by radio.

On a number of occasions we have called for assistance for motorists on the highway. We've asked other CB operators to phone the state police or a garage to get help. This is usually not necessary on our main roads, but in the back country you'd be surprised how much reassurance having a CB radio gives you.

It's also good to have CB when you are traveling with another party or in a caravan. If you need assistance, or if you just want to make a stop, you can pass the word directly . . . no problem.

170

It's best to get a CB set with twenty-three channels so that you will have the whole range. For twenty dollars you can get a five-year Class D license from the Federal Communications Commission, Gettysburg, Pa. 17325.

We also carry a set of small walkie-talkies, which do not require a license. If Olive and I go off fishing in different directions on a stream, we can stay in touch up to a mile or two. Many times when I have gone off by myself, she has called me on the CB set in the RV to tell me lunch was ready. Once I even called her to say I was bringing a fellow I met fishing on the river back to join us for dinner . . . she appreciated being warned in advance.

MORE TIPS

Locks on RV doors sometimes give trouble because they are in the weather at all times. An application of graphite into the keyholes and latches every so often will correct this problem. For some reason people have the idea that RV doors have to be slammed. It's really not necessary . . . which is a good thing to point out to the family.

Carry a small piece of beeswax or a candle to make drawers in the RV operate smoothly. Rub the runners and bases of drawers with the wax. While talking about wax, it's a good idea to keep the front of the vehicle covered with it. Wax makes the removal of bug splatter a simple job.

DITTY BAGS

There is something about man that leads me to suspect that we all have some squirrel blood in us. Every kitchen has a drawer that collects all kinds of junk from string to tools and many objects that will never be used. Try not to collect this sort of thing in your RV. If you must keep these treasures, keep filling that drawer at home. Still, some such objects are needed or have to be stored while traveling, so each person should have a "squirrel box" or a ditty bag for such possessions.

Some campsite areas abound in pine trees. This means that there are plenty of pine needles about. If the site is dusty from overuse have the kids gather some shopping bags full of pine needles and scatter them around your site. They will smell good, and they'll keep the dust down and prevent the grounds from getting muddy if it rains.

When you retire at night, be sure to put chairs and any other objects under the RV to keep them from getting covered with dew, unless you want to wash them. Don't leave any food outside unless you're trying to attract animals . . . they can be very destructive. Remember to instruct your family not to pick up or play with any wildlife they may encounter. The story of Bambi has been a disastrous one for the wildlife population. Many animals will have nothing to do with their young if they have the scent of man on them. We've all seen pictures of people feeding the black bears. Don't! Enjoy them from the other side of the glass windows.

Make sure your ax is sharp, but don't use it in a campsite before 7 A.M. Your neighbors might have had a rough night's sleep because your kids were raising the roof all night. If you are going to run a clothes line, be sure it's high enough so someone won't run into it at night. It's little things like these that will make your neighbor enjoy having you next door. Remember it's his vacation, too, and he's living closer to you in a campsite than your neighbor is at home.

If you are parked alone be sure to lock your door at night. There is no reason to unlock it and open the door, no matter who's outside. RVs should have an outside light at the door so you can see who is there. If someone wants to hold a conversation with you, do it through an open window. Pointing a flashlight through a window won't help you much. It'll light up the interior of your unit, and the reflection on the glass will prevent you from seeing out. If you do wish to see what's going on outside a motor home, have someone hold a flashlight against the window glass, then look from another window by cupping your hands around your eyes.

FIRST AID

It's always good to have someone in your party familiar with first aid. The problem with carrying a first-aid book is that many people become too excited and can't use the book. The Metropolitan Life Insurance Company has prepared a chart called "First Aid for the Family." It can be obtained free from any of their agents. It should be taped to the inside of a cabinet door for all to see. It's an alphabetical listing of the major problems that can arise. It covers such items as asphyxiation, bites, bleeding, burns, choking, convulsions, cuts, electric shock, eye injuries, falls, poisoning, stings, unconsciousness, and more. Explanations and instructions under each heading are short and to the point.

FIRST AID FOR THE LAND

Anti-pollution laws are getting more stringent, and they are being enforced. We won't say too much about this. We'll assume, like the preacher, that there is no use lecturing the folks in church about those who are not there. The rule of today's outdoor enthusiast has to be—if you can pack it in full, you can pack it out empty. Save yourself the cost of any fines, and remember that the land is your future, too.

OPTIONS . . . IT'S A LONG LIST AND EVERYONE HAS HIS OPINION

The optional features for an RV are many, and here is where a lot of money can be spent. It's important to consider each item carefully. One often makes a mistake because he has had no past experience. You do not want to load yourself down with useless gadgets, but at the same time you're going to want your comfort. The pocketbook may determine just how far you can go, but we hope our opinion will help you make some of your decisions.

Captain Marcy writes in his journal about those things that make life more pleasurable. The optional features he talks about are a little more basic than ours today. He presents five pages of drawings of folding chairs, tables, cots, and so on. He describes how to construct them and the materials to use. Today's manufacturers have these items all ready to go . . . for a price.

Our list was compiled from options listed by many manufacturers. It may not be possible to get some of these features on your particular recreation vehicle. Some apply to motor homes and not to trailers. Some of the items are discussed in detail elsewhere, but we feel that they are important enough to be listed again here. In addition, we would like to warn you about a few of the important automotive options, some of which should be explained more thoroughly by manufacturers.

TIRES

Tires were discussed elsewhere; they should be the biggest that will fit on the rims, heavy-duty truck type, and their tread should be the mud and snow variety. Belted radials have proven very successful. Some RVs come through equipped with a tread that will give problems off the main roads. Many manufacturers list the spare tire as an option; that's like making brains optional. In 1859 Captain Marcy suggested that oxen be used instead of mules for what we'd now call "off highway" travel. His reasoning was that if the worst came his travelers could eat the oxen. Possibly we should have Goodyear design a chocolate-flavored tire.

TIRE CARRIER

A tire carrier looks good, but on first glance it appears to be an option that could easily be eliminated from the list. Don't eliminate . . . buy. The standard carrier is usually under the chassis. The spare is slung underneath and held in place by a bracket. In case of a flat while on the road—and where else do they happen?—you'll appreciate a bumper carrier. It's a devil of a job to unload and load heavy tires while lying on your back under a vehicle.

174

Alternators are of various electrical outputs. Check to see what size alternator comes in your unit. RVs require a lot of electricity for appliances and lights. To stay out of battery trouble, you'll need a 60-amp alternator. Order it with your unit; it's like buying insurance.

ENGINES

Underpowered engines consume more gasoline than the big overpowered ones. This is contrary to your experience with automobiles, but it works this way with heavily laden motor homes. A 20-foot camper with a 318-cubic-inch engine may have all the power needed. The same-size engine, in a 20-foot motor home, will be sluggish because of all the extra weight. If the manufacturer gives you an option, it's because he feels the bigger engine will do the job better; but he offers the smaller engine to stay competitive in price. An engine that runs at a constantly high rpm will also sustain more wear and tear and consume more gas than a bigger engine running in its middle range. Too many motor homes huff and puff up long hills. Some are so slow that they can't get out of their own way. This can get on a traveler's nerves. Opt for the bigger engine; it'll cost less in the long run. If you plan to tow a boat or car behind a motor home, the bigger engine is a must.

SPEED CONTROL

Man has surely gotten lazy and loves his comfort. An optional autopilot or speed control can take much of the tension out of highway driving. With it, your vehicle will maintain a constant speed without any pressure on the accelerator pedal or any attention from the driver. This is a good device for a car towing a trailer or for the motor home. It allows the driver to concentrate on the road instead of the speedometer . . . and end the trip refreshed. The driver can shift position and come out of an eight-hour trip without the usual cramped right leg. It is actually a safety device, since the tension of long periods of high-speed driving is the cause of many accidents. It's an economy measure also. The prompt response of the automatic throttle control, operating on a governor principle, is a fuel saver.

To initiate the control, the driver accelerates until he reaches his desired speed. He then engages a switch on the instrument panel or on the turn-signal lever and takes his foot off the gas. A constant speed at that setting will be handled automatically from then on.

The driver can increase speed any time he wishes by using the accelerator; he can pass another car just as if the control were not in use. Then, when he removes his foot from the gas, the vehicle will return to the pre-set cruising speed. On the other hand, when the driver has to use the brake pedal, it automatically cuts out the speed control. After the slow-down, the gas pedal is used until the desired cruising speed is obtained, then the driver flips the switch and relaxes. Some models have a "resume" switch that'll bring the vehicle up to speed automatically. This optional feature costs only the price of a couple of tires, but it'll save a lot of wear and tear on the driver.

AUTOMOTIVE AIR-CONDITIONING

Once you have automotive air-conditioning, you'll never again do without it. It becomes as important as the heater is for winter travel. In the old days, Captain Marcy suggested:

> Start traveling at dawn and make a "nooning" during the heat of the day, as oxen and men suffer much from the heat of the sun in midsummer.

Air-conditioning lets you go any place at any time.

A roof-mounted air-conditioner is something the prairie traveler would have enjoyed. You will too. Units over twenty-four feet may need two 12,000 Btu units to do the job. This is determined more by the floor plan than the actual space. Units that are cut up into compartments are difficult to cool because of air flow. We'll have more to say about that and general ventilation later. It's needless to dwell on the comfort of air-conditioning; it's an optional feature that is a must in the Southwest and determined by the pocketbook in other parts of the country.

The automotive air-conditioner can be used in small units as a means of cooling the living quarters. This, however, means idling the engine in hot weather and throttling it up to keep it from over-heating. This is bad business: it's tough on the engine and it's not good having all that carbon monoxide floating around. The separate 110-volt air-conditioner for the living quarters is the best way to keep your cool.

TINTED GLASS

The new insulation materials in RV units are of the best. If it weren't for the windows and doors there would be little need for air-conditioning. Tinted glass is not needed along with air-conditioning. It does cut the heat of the sun, but everything you see outside is smoky colored. It's like seeing the world painted gray. It's not a very good feature in my book.

AWNINGS

The need for an awning depends on how you are going to use your RV. For those who are going to park and stay a while, an awning makes a fine patio. If you are off doing things like fishing during the height of the day, you'll find that you won't use it much: as the sun starts to pass over the yard arm, shade from the RV will be your patio area. If you are going to be more or less constantly on the move, awnings can be a headache.

Look what can be done with awnings. They're great if you're going to stay in one spot a long time. But they can be carried too far (*below*).

Nonautomotive air-conditioners need 110-volt AC current. They can be run from a hook-up with house current; and when that's not available, they can be operated off a self-contained generator. This is not a gadget but an expensive piece of heavy-duty machinery. Of course, as we have seen, there are more uses for a generator than just running the air-conditioner in the heat of the summer. Although it's about the most expensive piece of optional equipment on the list, a generator offers real self-sufficiency. Even the manufacturers haven't as yet recognized the full potential of the power plant. We have some friends who live all year round in their motor home. The only thing the wife refused to give up when they sold their house was the electric organ. It's now installed in the back bedroom of their motor home.

Generators come in all sizes. The smallest that is practical for running an air-conditioner puts out 2500 watts. This size, because of its single-phase engine, is noisier than the 4000- and 5000-watt units. The noise level of the latter two is very low, at least for the occupants of the RV, for whom the sound-proofing is very good; but there is an outside problem. The noise level can disturb people in nearby campsites, so some parks request that you not use your generator.

All the comforts of home. The organ was part of her life so it went along.

HOUR METER

Generators must be serviced after varying numbers of hours of running, instead of by miles like an automotive engine. Since they are run on an odd schedule, a clock is used to determine when it's time for an oil change and maintenance. An hour meter is a must in conjunction with the power plant. It's a dash-mounted clock that starts when the generator is switched on and automatically stops when it's turned off. It's an easy way to record the accumulated running time.

One manufacturer made a survey of power-plant owners and found that many used their generators only for the air-conditioner. Possibly they hadn't thought of using them for outside lights for a patio party or for the hundreds of other uses of electricity.. The section on winter living gives you a fuller understanding of how the electricity can be used.

WIRING INSTALLATION FOR A POWER PLANT

If you decide not to buy the generator at first, keep the option open by ordering your unit with factory installation of the necessary wiring and gasoline connection for a generator. This option is offered, and it will save a big expense if you put the power plant in at a later date.

BATTERY CHARGER, COMBINATION WITH CONVERTER

This is a good device because it means that when you use the generator you will automatically be charging the batteries. It's even wise to install a second portable charger of about 8 amps along with the built-in one. See the section on winter living. The faster you can bring the batteries back to full potential, the better. Check to see if this is standard equipment or offered optionally.

EXHAUST FAN

One reason why air-conditioning is needed in many of the RV vehicles is that the ventilation is not as good as it should be. This is especially true in units that have sliding windows. The big areas of glass can fool you. Usually the larger windows are constructed with a center section that is stationary. The smaller sections on each side open, but since they slide on a common track these windows will open only half of their width. This is inadequate on a hot day. Electric-fan roof vents are important optional features. They help move air. It's advisable to install one in the bathroom. Its function is double: it clears the steam out after a shower and will also help general circulation. For anyone who is allergic to tobacco smoke, a roof vent in the lounge area is a blessing. It'll draw the smoke off as fast as it's generated. Some roof vents are of the all-weather variety. They can be opened in rain or snow without the unit getting wet inside. If this isn't the kind offered optionally by the factory, don't order it. Have your dealer obtain and install the all-weather-type vent.

A powered stove hood and vent are well worth the price and

should be ordered from the factory. They help ventilation and eliminate cooking smells which are really appreciated only *before* a meal.

A combination escape hatch and vent in the roof is becoming a very popular optional feature. It will move plenty of air, since it's big enough for a person to climb through. It can also save your life in case of an accident when the vehicle falls over on its side and the door is blocked. All vents of this type come with screens.

An escape hatch is a good safety feature.

A screen door is optional in some units. Of course, this is a necessary thing to have for summer. While talking about screening, it seems well to point out that the units that have the window screening on the inside of the glass windows are best. Many units are made with the screens outside. Their designers should be forced to take their wives out in such a unit. The road mud and dirt collect in the screening and make it almost impossible to see out. The screens have to be removed to clean them . . . not a job to be done at a fast gas stop. In the winter, snow and ice collect between the outside screens and the windows. This kind of designing is thoughtless. This picture taken in the snow shows what happens.

Screening should be on the inside. Otherwise snow or road mud collects in the mesh and presents a constant problem while traveling. That is bad designing.

REAR WIPER AND WASHER

Motor homes create a suction and drag that scoop all the muck off the road and deposit it on the rear window. A rear-window washer and wiper, therefore, will pay for itself in the first rain. Anything to keep the rear window clean in bad weather is an excellent piece of optional equipment. In bad weather the truck-type side mirrors become fogged and useless. Rear vision will be important under such conditions.

MUSIC AND TV

Radios, TV, and tapes are a matter of individual taste. A lot of families use their RV as a way of getting away from the TV. For those who need it along, a directional, collapsible antenna can be installed on the roof; also, some companies offer a swivel shelf inside for the TV. A rechargeable TV can be used, or one can be run directly off a plug-in or the generator. We have friends who carry a TV but have no antenna. The kids have to find someplace else to plug it in . . . pretty smart.

The combination of AM-FM radio and a tape deck is a good investment. If you have the option of four speakers, take it. These speakers are controlled in pairs, and you can adjust the sound.

Tape cassettes are always scattered about. We bought a cassette holder, then made a rack for it under the tape player. No more hunting!

 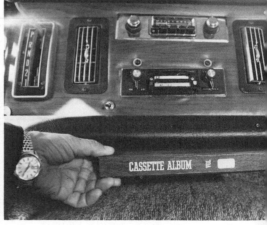

Either the stereo or monaural can be controlled to fill the whole vehicle with music, even if it's soft. If you do not like the quality of the AM programs, you should include FM in the package. A cassette tape deck rounds out the system; then you can have the music of your choice when you can't pull it in by radio. Many manufacturers do not offer the cassette tape but do offer the eight-track system instead. Media people say this system is on the way out; the cassette system is more versatile. You can make your own tapes on a home set and play them on the RV player. We're going to hear a lot more in the future about taped travel tours. You'll be able to rent or buy cassettes and hear a lecture tour as you drive along . . . that'll complete your programed living!

BUNKS

There are all kinds of bunk options available. Which one you choose is something you will have to figure out to meet your own family needs. Be sure to see and measure the bunks you are considering buying. What some makers consider sleeping arrangements for two would be perfectly adequate for midgets.

If you do not take all the bunks offered optionally, ask for cabinets in those places. Some designers place the cabinets around the upper walls so that in the rear of a unit they can install either a bunk bed or cabinets. (They neglect to point out that they design the area so that either choice will mean easy installation for them.) Since a bed is so much wider than the cabinets are deep, if you choose the rear cabinets, valuable space on the side walls is wasted. They'll put cabinets across the back but not extra ones on the side walls. So, if you want the ceiling cabinets instead of the extra rear bunk, order extra cabinets to fill the wasted space on each side wall.

BUNK LADDERS

Ladders are bulky and hard to store in the daytime. There are ways of getting around buying one. Often one step is enough to get the person up. In that case, if a folding boat-step can be fastened to a wall it can solve the problem cheaply. A rope ladder, even if it's homemade, will also do the job. It can be hung from the bed and is easy to store. A full step-ladder will be necessary only for older folks.

BOLSTERS

Although bolsters are offered optionally by many makers, they really are a necessity. In the daytime, beds convert to couches. They are too deep for sitting. The bolsters make it possible to sit back and be comfortable. Sorry, you'll have to buy them.

CARPETS AND RUGS

Don't take the rug option if it's at all possible to avoid doing so. (See Rugs and Carpets, pages 74–75.) Some manufacturers offer a tile floor as standard covering. Take it and install your own covering. If you do not have this choice and must take carpeting, do not select the shag variety, for the reasons already explained.

GAS FURNACE

Gas furnaces come with different Btu outputs, and in some the blower system is optional. Be sure the system you select has a blower. Without it you'll have unevenly heated quarters. Heat rises and can leave your feet awfully cold. As for size, furnaces for the larger RVs are commonly available with either 23,000 Btu or 30,000 Btu input. Theoretically, both should burn the same amount of bottled gas if they are thermostatically controlled. If you expect to use your RV as a ski lodge, the bigger heater makes a lot of sense. If you expect to travel to only moderately cold areas, the 23,000 Btu unit will do fine.

186

Some large RV units need more than one heater. Sometimes this is provided by a second small 11,000-Btu unit, the kind common in small trailers or conversion vans. It can do the job very well if the area it has to heat is not too large. It's wise to check on just how the heating ducts have been laid out in a unit. We have seen some units with very large lounge areas up front, but the whole forward area was devoid of any heating outlets.

Some of the smaller units are using a combination stove, oven, and forced-air heater. It is safe and would make an excellent back-up for the main heater in a large RV. The top of the unit operates like any four-burner LP stove. It has a thermostatically controlled, sealed combustion chamber and a ducting system that heats the air at the floor. The combustion fumes are vented outside. The combination costs little more than an ordinary stove.

TANKS . . . EXTRA CAPACITY

It's a good idea to opt for the biggest bottled-gas tanks your unit will hold. The LP gas system should always have two tanks, one as a back-up. Twenty-pound tanks are standard. The storage compartment will usually take thirty-pound tanks or bigger. It's well worth the difference to get the larger size; it's like carrying an extra tank. An automatic switch-over valve, previously mentioned, is an inexpensive item, and a must. Your first tank may run out in the middle of the night. With the automatic change valve, the second tank takes over, raising its red flag to signal that one tank is empty. Now you'll have the time to get that first tank refilled and gas flow has not been interrupted.

Opt for the extra water tank; you can never have enough. (See the section on water, pages 90–95. It'll scare you into buying the water purifier, too. For certain areas it's a must.)

An extra gasoline tank will eventually pay for itself because you can fill it up where the price is right and drive through the high-priced areas without buying gas. Separate tanks are a good idea if you have a power generator on board. It'll draw gasoline from only one of the tanks. The extra tank will end worry about running out of gasoline while parked and generating electricity. Generators use about half a gallon an hour.

220-AMPERE BATTERY

As previously mentioned, the battery delivered with units for the household part of the RV is usually a heavy-duty job putting out 70 amps. It's a good idea to exchange it for the bigger 220-amp battery offered optionally. With all your appliances, you're going to need it. For example, the blower on the furnace is driven by an electric motor that draws 7 amps. That does not sound like much, but in ten hours of operation it'll completely drain a 70-amp battery, and that's not considering any other electrical appliances, such as lights, that you might use.

Of course there should be a second separate battery for the automotive needs.

REFRIGERATORS

The usual, standard refrigerator equipment is of four-cubic-feet storage capacity. Refrigerators come in sizes up to eight cubic feet. Don't decide on this on the basis of your home experience. Here is a place to save. We've fed four big eaters out of a four-cubic-footer on many a trip. It's all in the way you pack the food. (See the section on refrigerators, pages 81–90.)

TOILETS

There are usually three or more types of toilets optionally available, and after much consideration, we have stayed with the standard toilet that comes with all units. Here is where you can save a lot of money and possibly some headaches. Nothing much can go wrong with a marine-type, fresh-water, flush john. (See the section on toilets, pages 96–100.)

MOTOR-AID WATER HEATER

This optional feature, discussed on page 116, is one that very few manufacturers offer. It's very convenient, and if you ski it is more than a luxury.

TRAILER HITCH

If you expect to use a trailer hitch make sure you stipulate when ordering that you want the necessary wiring and connectors. This may sound stupid, but with many makers the hitch does not include the electrical hook-up.

WATER-LEVEL GAUGE

If you have a fresh-water pressure system you need this item, but the problem is that most manufacturers install such poor quality gauges that they are not accurate. I thought it was just our particular gauge that was at fault until I spoke to a lot of other RVers. The electric-plate-type gauge is best and is usually standard in only the most expensive units.

SEPTIC TANK-LEVEL GAUGE

If this item comes with the unit, that's fine, but a septic tank-level gauge is not worth the expense of having it specially installed.

CURTAINS

Special curtains are offered optionally in some units. These offers are worth examining. Make sure you have wraparound windshield curtains in the driving area. Sometimes these cost extra. The driver's night curtain will give you the privacy needed but it cuts off the whole cab area.

MEDICINE CABINET

Take this optional feature if it doesn't come with the unit. The cabinet should incorporate a light for shaving. It's a necessary storage place for medicines, toilet items, and cosmetics. Besides, you'll need a mirror in the bathroom.

THE DRIVER'S AREA

Sun visors, armrests, and headrests usually are offered optionally. Although they make the driving and co-pilot chairs as comfortable as any in your living room, you'll have to try them to see if you want to spend the extra money for these attachments. A double co-pilot seat, available at extra cost, is also a very comfortable arrangement for either one or two people.

The best kind of sun visors are those made of colored plexiglass. They temper the brilliance of the sun without cutting down the area of vision. The driver should also have convex sideview mirrors on each side of the vehicle. These prevent visual dead spots along the side of the unit where you can't see small cars. Many times in foggy weather, when the flat truck mirrors no longer reflect clearly because they're covered by a film of water, the convex mirrors will still function.

The double co-pilot seat is excellent. It's very comfortable.

ROOF, BAGGAGE RACK, AND LADDER

Optional features are a ladder by which to reach the roof of your motor home, and a rail around the roof to which luggage, skis, or what-not can be attached for carrying. Order these features by all means. Aside from the great convenience of carrying things on it, the roof makes a fine vantage point for sports events, photography, or sun bathing. In good weather you'll find many uses for it. I'm sure that if Captain Marcy had this option he'd want to post a sentry on top of the unit to watch for Indians.

WARRANTIES . . . WHAT YOU SHOULD KNOW

My purpose in discussing warranties is not to frighten you off as a potential buyer of a motor home, but to open your eyes to the problems that can arise. The first things that should be discussed in the manufacturer's warranty are the chassis and the basic running parts of the motor home. In this respect a warranty on a motor home is the same as on a car.

This photograph showing thousands of motor-home chassis in the lot behind the Winnebago Company's plant in Iowa is really included for the benefit of automotive executives who may be reading this book. There are literally acres of Dodge chassis here. The camera could have been pointed in any one of the 360 degrees and it would have pictured chassis from close-up to infinity. I was told when I took this picture that, for that particular year, motor-home chassis made the difference between profit and loss for the Dodge truck division.

Chassis manufacturers seem to have very little control over their dealers. The extent of the service the local auto dealer will provide is a matter of whether or not he wants to cooperate. His attitude can be that he didn't sell the motor home and he has enough problems with his own customers. There is not much the public can do about this attitude. But if the company wants the profit it has to assume the service responsibility.

The large manufacturers are recognizing this problem and are trying to set up centers to handle RV service, but they are moving too slowly. The industry is growing faster than their service centers. It's like owning a foreign car and having limited service available.

It's a good idea to get this problem worked out before you plunk down the hard-earned cash. Many motor-home dealers are not automotive dealers and do not have facilities for warranty work on the chassis . . . and in like manner, those dealers who can service the motor wouldn't know how to repair a faulty toilet.

Once you work out the problem of servicing the chassis in your home locale, you should be sure that the RV dealer can handle the home appliances in the unit. It's a good idea to go through his shop and see if he at least looks as though he knew what he was doing. Talk to some of his customers who come in for service and see if they are satisfied. Some dealers flatly and honestly say they only sell and do no servicing. They may offer you a good purchase price, but don't buy unless you can do the work yourself.

If you are on the road and need service, check the prices before the work starts. Some dealers take the attitude that they are doing you a favor and since you own a very expensive unit you can surely pay a fancy price for their work.

A motor home is a rather complicated piece of machinery. Someday manufacturers will be just as self-sufficient as they advertise their units to be. They will make their own chassis and all the appliances inside the house. Plans for this are on the drawing board, but it's still way off in the future. As things are now, even the biggest RV companies are just assemblers. They buy air-conditioners, heaters, refrigerators, toilets, and what-not on the open market. The problem with this, as far as the customer is concerned, is many-fold. Who is responsible for the appliances? You really have your hook only into the guy who is selling you the unit. He should be responsible to you for any major problem. This should be put in writing; and the period of his responsibility should be a full year.

The full year is necessary because a problem that develops in the winter won't show up until summer, and vice versa. Let me give you an example.

We went skiing and parked at the foot of a slope with another motor home. As soon as we arrived, the owner of the other RV came over and asked if I knew anything about gas heaters. He had a serious problem. His pilot light worked, but he couldn't make the main burner go on. With the weather we were having, this was no joke. Night was coming on, and the wind-chill factor was 50 degrees below zero. It stayed that cold for the next twenty-four hours. It was so cold and the wind was so high that we never did go skiing for fear of frostbite.

Needless to say, we tried everything we knew, but it wasn't enough to repair his unit. We finally emptied out his fresh-water system to prevent a freeze-up. The family tried to get into a motel, but there was no space available and they were too tired to start the drive home. They survived the cold by running the automotive heater every so often during the night. We reminded them not to use the burners on the stove for heat . . . that could use up their oxygen supply.

194

Next morning we had Jim and his wife and kids in for breakfast and some good warm air. The wife fought back the tears as she told her husband that he should sell the motor home and buy a boat, which she had wanted in the first place. He argued back that she couldn't blame Open Road, the maker, for the problem with the Coleman heater. She answered, "We didn't buy a Coleman. We bought a motor home with heat!"

These folks had never before used their new motor home during the winter. They had bought their unit in the fall, and during that season all worked well. So it was five months before they ran into their first problem.

When I got home from that aborted ski trip it was still bitterly cold. We emptied the motor home, turned off the heater, and went to bed. Next day I went out to the unit to do some work in it and decided to fire up the furnace. I ran into the exact same problem Jim had. The pilot light worked, but the main burner refused to go on when I turned up the thermostat. I fiddled with all the wires. I checked them out for continuity and did all the same things that I had tried for him. Just before I announced to my wife that the next weekend's trip was off because I'd have to get the heater repaired, I sat down in my very cold motor home to try to think the whole thing out.

I had an idea, and I decided to give it a try. I pointed an infra-red lamp into the heater compartment. The furnace still didn't work. Then I took the cover off the thermostat and heated it, and I gave the thermostat a tap with my finger. The furnace went on. My problem was solved that easily . . . the on-and-off switch in the thermostat was frozen.

Now, I don't profess to be a one-man research center, but I decided to try the whole thing again. I found that in extremely cold weather the spring that made the electrical connection when the thermostat was in the on position would not work. Tapping it with a pencil or applying heat made it function. I called Jim to tell him of my discovery. He had a similar story. They had gone over a rut on the way home; it jarred the unit, and the heater went on.

Having spent many years as a research chemist, even I must admit that this is not a big enough sample to draw any final conclusion from, but two out of two looks suspicious. Was this thermostat design ever tested in bitterly cold weather? Obviously not. The appliance industry is growing so fast that production seems to be more important to them than testing under all conceivable conditions. The heater's unreliability is just one example of this problem.

As I tell the next story, you may get the feeling that I am out to crucify the Coleman Company. That is not so. It just so happens that my experiences have been with their products because they are the manufacturers of most of the appliances in my recent units.

This story begins on the road. We had had our unit for only a few months, and on the first blistering hot day that year we were on Interstate 80 going through Pennsylvania. I wasn't completely satisfied with the way the air-conditioner was working and thought I'd like to have it checked out. A listing of authorized dealers for every state in the Union comes with every appliance. We checked our list and found we were coming to a town that had an authorized service center. We got off the highway in Clearfield, Pennsylvania, to find its proprietor. It took the better part of an hour to locate him, only to be told that his was only a Coleman-heater service center, and he knew nothing about the air-conditioner. He could give us no explanation of why he was listed in their service manual as being an authorized air-conditioning repair service. That was surely an hour wasted, but not the end of the story.

At the first sign of fall I ran into a very minor problem. I noted that the pilot light on my Coleman heater was burning yellow instead of blue. It's no simple job to get at the pilot light to clean the orifice, so I decided a mechanic should do it. This time, instead of going to my dealer, I decided to go directly to the manufacturer's authorized service people. I frankly wanted the experience of finding out how my warranty was going to work.

From the list of sales and service centers which came with my now six-month-old unit, I was first shocked to see that there was only one listing for my state, but I was pleased to find that it was located within an hour's drive. I called the number and asked for Mr. Stone (which isn't his right name). The woman who answered was extremely upset. I tried to explain to her about my pilot problem and then she told me her problem.

"Mr. Stone isn't here. He hasn't been here for two years. I never met the man. This is my number now and I don't know how to fix your heater, and nobody else in Wappinger Falls, New York, knows how to fix the bloody things either."

I tried to excuse myself, saying I was sorry. She went on, "I get calls night and day and I wish the Coleman Company would get someone else in town to answer their phone." She hung up.

The thing that disturbed me, besides upsetting the poor woman, was that Coleman still listed someone who had been out of business two years. Didn't they update their list?! They have all purchasers of their product listed in their warranty file. Couldn't they send new lists out as service centers change?

Now, it appeared from my listing that I had no one in my state as a representative of the company. But I heard that there was a very good repairman in a town nearby. I took the motor home to him. It only took an hour for him to get at the dirty part. When he put the heater back together and started it up he didn't like the sound of the unit. He took it apart again and found a defective main valve. When reassembled, it still wasn't working to his satisfaction; he took it apart again and found a broken thermocouple and a shorted-out switch. He didn't have those parts, so it cost me over sixty dollars in labor charges just to find out what was wrong.

I wrote a letter to Coleman, not mentioning that I was going to write a book about living on wheels. I figured that if they knew I was going to do a book they would go out of their way to get my problem solved. I wanted them to respond as if I were an ordinary customer. I also sent a copy of the letter. to the manufacturer of my motor home.

I received two responses.

Mr. Jones, the president of Coleman, passed my letter down the line, and I received a letter ignoring the fact that the service center listings were wrong. They did send me a new, up-to-date list. They sent me a check for $32.92 to cover my cost of $62.92, saying that the charge for labor was too high. But I still had a heater that was not working.

The copy of the letter that went to the manufacturer of the motor home brought a better response. They sent a completely new heater and asked me to return the defective one. I had the new one installed for twenty-five dollars. My total out-of-pocket cost for what had started as a simple problem was fifty-five dollars.

Later, when I met some of the management of the Coleman Company at a national recreation vehicle show, I told them the story. They knew then that I was writing a book and asked what they could do. I told them "Nothing."

The warranty problem does get complicated, because of that man in between the maker of the appliance and the customer—the manufacturer of the final vehicle. In the case of the defective furnace, the repairman had discovered a short in a switch. This turned out not to be Coleman's mistake. It had occurred during installation at Winnebago. Throughout their whole electrical assembly process, Winnebago uses a certain kind of plastic and metal connector. Coleman does not use these connectors. The troublesome switch was mistakenly shorted out with one of the Winnebago connectors. For that defective part the appliance maker couldn't be held responsible. Who is responsible for total labor charges and other defective parts like the broken thermocouple? The customer should not have to worry about whether it was broken before it left the original factory or whether it was broken during installation. Your dealer has to be responsible for any such defect. But also, these units are used for travel. You have to be protected on the road against malfunctioning of your chassis, your appliances, or your over-all unit. All concerned with the manufacturing process should take heed.

I asked one RVer what he would do if he had to do it all over again. His answer was a surprise. He said that first, before he signed the papers and took delivery, he'd park the unit on the dealer's lot and run all appliances for two days to make sure they were working. "Then I'd give it a hose test," he went on to say. He explained it this way: "The only problem I ever had with my unit showed up in the first rain storm; I had two leaky windows. Everything else has been fine—the heater, refrigerator, toilet, you name it—but those leaky windows caused all kinds of trouble. We drove down the road wringing out towels. We finally got the problem solved. But next time I buy, I'm going to get a hose and shoot a hard stream of water around the windows. If they leak, I won't take delivery until they reset and caulk them."

The moral of this story is that these units have become so sophisticated that it's like buying a house. A brand new $60,000 home could still have a roof leak, caused by a nail costing one penny. It's the builder's responsibility to correct the trouble. Your RV dealer stands in the position of the builder. Make sure he is carrying out his responsibility for making any necessary repairs. Indeed, the RV dealer has an even greater responsibility than the builder. He's got to stand behind not only the chassis but also the furnishings and appliances in the vehicle and the motor equipment that moves it down the road.

INSURANCE . . . PROTECT YOURSELF

The new craze for living on wheels is causing as much stir today in insurance circles as the introduction of the horseless carriage did at the turn of the century. Many agents today don't know the difference between a stationary mobile home and a motor home, but they are learning fast. Many companies are still hesitant to write insurance on motor homes because they are not used to dealing in value figures for a vehicle ranging from $20,000 up to $40,000. But this is a good market for the insurance companies. Every year more and more of them are getting into RV coverage. Some will write insurance on an RV as a favor to long-term good customers. This kind of coverage may be the easiest for a new RVer to arrange, but it's not always the best choice. It's advisable to use companies that specialize in this field. Here are some who have been in it the longest: Foremost in Grand Rapids, Michigan; Traveler's Bancorporation in Estherville, Iowa; and J. E. Wells in Los Angeles, California. Wells does most of its business in the West. Safeco of

Seattle, Washington, writes nationwide. Many other companies are inviting the RV business.

Now, what kind of insurance do you need on your motor home? You should have the kind you have on your car, plus more. Make sure your company and agent know this RV game. Because motor homes are mounted on truck chassis, the owner sometimes ends up with a high-priced policy for a commercial truck. Today's motor-

This is my motor home. How much would you pay for insurance? I called my regular auto insurance agent and he quoted me a price of $384 a year. He said it was his company's commercial rate. Exactly the same insurance was obtained from an RV specialist for $118 a year. It pays to check price before you insure.

home policy should provide combination automotive and trailer coverage. Make sure you carry coverage of at least $100,000 for one person injured in one accident; $300,000 for more than one person injured in an accident; and $25,000 for property damage liability. This doesn't cost very much more than the minimum requirements for your state, but the minimum coverage could have you in trouble if you are hauled into court.

There is a new feature being tried by some of the companies. If you use your vehicle less than a stipulated number of days, say less than 100 per year, your premium is much lower.

Some insurance policies provide for coverage in only forty-eight states. It's best to have world coverage; Alaska and Canada, at least, should be included. Be sure to ask about this so you will know what you are getting. As far as Mexico is concerned, some companies write policies that are "good" for 100 miles below the border. Don't count on this coverage; it could be worthless. Never, but *never,* go into Mexico without buying special Mexican insurance from a bona fide agent. These agents can be found at all border gateways. Be sure the insurance is Mexican approved. Mexico has some crazy laws. In one case all the occupants of an

South of the Border

RV went to jail and the vehicle was impounded after an accident in which no other vehicle except the RV was involved. The driver in this case had world-wide coverage with his American company, but try to explain that to the Mexican *policia*.

Canada is not as much of a problem. Before you cross the border your American agent will have a special card issued for you.

If you are going to rent a trailer or motor home, have your agent check the protection the owner has for you. You should get the policy endorsed to cover the rental or go to your own company and add the vehicle onto your automobile coverage.

Check to see if the policy covers personal effects. Such coverage may be limited to a stipulated amount. Full coverage can be obtained with an additional payment, if you wish.

When buying insurance, note that there is a difference between an actual cash-value policy and a replacement policy. After the vehicle is a few years old its value drops, but to replace it could have you digging deep. Many companies offer this feature at very little extra cost; in some cases it's no more expensive at all.

If you are insuring a trailer, make sure all the coverage applies when the trailer is detached from the towing vehicle. Check to see if the number of wheels on your trailer has anything to do with your insurance. In some cases four-wheel trailers require special coverage. Ask before you buy the insurance whether the policy covers glass breakage and the furnishings that come built into the unit. If you plan to tow something behind a motor home, will it be covered on the original policy?

Remember that these companies don't have to renew your policy the next year and if you have more than one violation or accident a year, they may refuse to cover you . . . so drive with care.

ANIMALS . . . PETS OR PESTS?

Traveling with animals can be fun or it can be disaster. Having written three dog-training books, I have received much mail on the subject of travel. The problems range from overexcited dogs to car sickness.

These problems practically always stem from the fact that the animals were started traveling too late. We always begin training our dogs to travel at a very early age. By the eighth week they get their first trip to town in the car. From the beginning they are put in a wire kennel in the station wagon or motor home, even for short trips. The wire kennel allows them to see you and smell you and it also keeps them in their place. If they're started early enough they won't have a sickness problem, which is really caused by nervousness. If your dog has this problem it's because he has come to dislike the car. Play with him in the parked car; then try it with the engine running . . . he'll learn it's not so bad.

The dog that's a yapper can be taught to settle down by learning the lesson himself. We'll take a pup to a strange parking place. Of course he'll want to leave the car when we do. By leaving him in the car kennel and letting him bark his head off, he'll soon get tired, learn that the barking didn't do a bit of good, and go to sleep. Don't return to the car until he's quiet, or he'll get the impression that the barking brought you back.

One fact you should know about dogs; they love a cave. It has been that way with them for millions of years. Why do you think they go behind a chair to sleep? It's a place where they feel safe and secure. A kennel gives them the same sense of security. We give them such a place in our motor home . . . and here is why.

A wet or dirty dog in an RV can be a real problem. Indeed, shortage of space alone is a reason to keep them from underfoot. There's a solution to all this that has proven very successful for both the family and the dogs. We convert a space, either under the sink or in a big-enough cabinet at floor level, into a kennel. A doorway is provided by cutting through the outside wall. The new door is made of insulated material. This gives our two dogs their own entrance and exit. On the inside we remove the cabinet door,

The kennel door locks from the outside. A step makes the jump up easy for the old dog. When the dogs are inside, a screen keeps out the insects. We had always built in such an arrangement. In this unit we had the maker do it.

cut out its center, and replace it with a decorative wire screening. The dogs are very happy in such a kennel. They can hear, see, and smell us. If we want them inside the house with us, they can come in when we open the inside door.

The outside door is a little complicated to make. It's really composed of two doors. The outer one is closed and locked when traveling. When we are parked, in good weather, this outer door is opened. A wire kennel door is installed inside the outer door, so the dogs can get plenty of air. A nylon insect netting is snapped over the kennel door to keep the flies out.

The accompanying pictures show a step-up to the outside kennel door. One of our dogs is getting old and he can't jump that high any more. The step makes it easy for him to get in and out. Both dogs enjoy their kennel. This has been their way of life and they like traveling as much as we do. With that outside door open we never have to lock our RV. The sight of two big black dogs inside the unit is all the protection we need.

Guests are always surprised, after they have been in our unit for some time, to learn that we have dogs aboard . . . that's how quiet they are.

Many people travel with their cats. They are not as much of a problem. However, cats, too, should be trained to travel at an early

age. Make it a way of life for them and they will be good travelers. Sleeping quarters are up to you. A small kennel can be made in a cabinet if you don't want the cat loose at night. A litter box will solve housebreaking problems. A plastic container in the kennel is the best. A small electric exhaust fan will take care of any odor. A flexible hose can be used from the fan, through the wall to the outside.

It's good to train a cat to walk on leash when it's young. This will solve some of your camping problems. Your animals are your responsibility. Don't let them become someone else's headache. Check before you go to campsites with animals; some places do not allow them. Of course the reason is that a lot of folks before you didn't take care of their pets. Don't just put a dog out to be in someone else's way. Buy a swivel dog tender. It's screwed into the ground and has a swivel top to attach a chain or rope. Before you retire at night, hook it up and put the chain next to the door. Then when you get up, all you have to do is hook up the dog and put him out.

The term "recreation vehicle" is in some ways a misnomer—eating, sleeping, dressing, and so on can't be considered recreation. They are the things we must do whether it's a work day or a play day. We've tried to show you how to do these necessary chores under the best possible circumstances and with the least amount of work. The vehicle, then, is a way to go; it's the means to the recreation.

What you are really buying in a motor home is flexibility and mobility, without losing the comforts of our everyday life. The statistics show that this kind of living is catching on, fast. Although the motor-home industry is in its infancy, already state, federal, and private campground facilities are being overtaxed to meet the needs of this fast-growing life-style. The biggest growth is, and will continue to be, in the area of private campsites.

Flexibility is really the key to the whole RV game. You can go almost anywhere you want; the choice is yours. Many families use their units in conjunction with other activities. They'll stay on the property of friends or at the site of a specific sporting event. These people know where they are going and they carry their sporting equipment with them.

Where do you park if you are simply touring? This is perhaps the question most asked by folks just starting out. There are many answers. If it is a long-distance trip, the best places for overnight stops naturally depend upon the area. In the large cities it's possible to stay in outdoor parking lots. If you do not want to go into the heart of the city, you can stay in some rest areas along the super-highways. Pull up to where the trucks stop for the night; close the curtains and go to bed. On many occasions you'll find when you stop for gas that you've had enough driving right then and there. On such occasions, ask the attendant if it's O.K. to park behind the station and catch some sleep. Lock the door and turn in. Shopping centers can also be used for a night's stay on long trips.

Many towns welcome traveling families. They have areas set aside for just such overnight parking. Some towns, however, are against this sort of thing. They will have signs announcing that no street parking is permitted between certain night-time hours. Even at such places, if you ask, you'll find that they do have an area where you won't be disturbed. The hippie movement inspired many local laws against overnight parking. We have been to resort areas where the campsites have been full and the "No Parking" signs were posted all over town, but we had no trouble in the local park. We were told that the law really applied to "them hippies who didn't have any money to spend in town." Many towns are discovering that the people who come to stay in recreation vehicles have money to spend, and that is always welcome. Make it a point to ask where you can stay.

The kind of traveling flexibility we are talking about doesn't mean you start out blindly and travel into new areas without any planning. It can be done that way, but you could be missing a lot. A family we know tells the story of how they discovered their favorite state park. One night they stopped to sleep, and next morning they discovered that they had slept near a sign giving directions to a state campsite. For fun, they went to see the place they had missed . . . and they've been going there ever since.

There are many listings and sources of campground locations. *Woodall's Trailer Parks and Campgrounds,* published by the Woodall Publishing Co., 500 Hyacinth Place, Highland Park, Ill. 60035, is the most complete. It lists, state by state, every park and campground, whether it be private, public, municipal, county, state, or national. The publishers send their regional representatives to evaluate the campgrounds. They cross-index their listings and provide colored maps, besides giving directions for reaching each campsite.

Woodall's uses a rating system that shows what its investigator thought of each campground; it lists available facilities and activities and the dates the campgrounds are open. This book is the size of the phone directory for New York City. There are all kinds of good information in it. The campground ads alone are worth the $5.95 price.

The other book you should have is the *Rand McNally Road Atlas.* It's available for $2.95 at newsstands or by writing to Rand McNally & Co., P.O. Box 7600, Chicago, Ill. 60680. It shows the major and secondary roads all the way from Central America up to northern Canada and Alaska.

Every traveler should know about the Golden Eagle Passport issued by the United States government. It costs $10.00 and is your annual permit to use the more than 3,000 recreational areas operated by five different federal agencies. It can be purchased by writing to the Bureau of Outdoor Recreation, P.O. Box 7763, Washington, D.C. 20044.

Some of the finest places in America for stopping overnight or longer are found in our national parks. A complete list can be obtained from the National Park Service, Washington, D.C. 20246.

Motel chains, too, are now trying to attract the RVers. Motel operators are starting to see that many of the RVers are really no different from the car travelers. One carries his bed and gear and the other rents it when he arrives. But both want meals, drinks, attractive lawns, and swimming pools when they get to their destinations. In many of the resort areas the motels are building screened-off hook-ups to provide all the needs of the RVer. The price of the hook-up includes the use of the recreational facilities in the area. This is really the best of two worlds.

FRANCHISE CAMPGROUNDS

The franchise campground business is not new. Outfits like KOA (Kampgrounds of America) have over 500 sites in the United States and Mexico. Unlike the motels, which already have all the facilities, the proprietors of these campgrounds start from a piece of land and construct all the necessary buildings, stores, washrooms, recreation halls, and facilities for sports. You're welcome at these campgrounds either as an overnighter or to stay a while.

The success of such ventures as Timber Shores, a campground on Grand Traverse Bay in Michigan, has shown just how elegant and successful this kind of living can be. They offer swimming, tennis, golf, dance bands, and even social directors. You can go out to dine at the campground restaurant or have dinner delivered by

208

the camp's own catering service. It's much the same as a fine resort hotel except for the price, six to nine dollars a day.

Holiday Inns, the motel people, have seen the potential in this business and expect to have 300 to 400 campgrounds within the next few years. They are being run under the name Trav-L-Parks and offer free reservation service through the motel operation. Ramada Inns have started their franchise camping operations. Gateway Sporting Goods hopes to have fifty Holiday Camps operating shortly. The list could go on.

It is not our purpose to give listings of information, since *Woodall's* is a storehouse of all you'll want to know, and they revise it every year. We're trying to show you the various ways you can go. Even tent campers do their thing in different ways. The backpacker goes off by himself and lives alone with his environment. Another group of campers pitches tents so close to one another that they could use common tent pegs. This living is pretty much the same as apartment living in a big city. One type of person likes to be alone and another likes to be with people. Most of us fall somewhere between these two extremes. Who is to say who is having more fun? The RVers are really no different from any other group of people. Some like to go into the back country and live by themselves and others like the social aspects of campgrounds, beaches, and the like. RV rallies are very popular. These are sponsored by many different associations. *Woodall's* lists them. Many of the large RV manufacturers have their own clubs. They stage annual rallies and owners come from all over the country just for the sociability of it all. The clubs break down into state and local organizations that have weekend get-togethers.

Summer rally, Burlington, Vermont

Many of these clubs, as well as commercial organizations, sponsor "caravans"—tours on which a number of private vehicles travel as a group. They can be anything from a two-week journey into Canada or Mexico to a year's trip around the world. Each family lives and travels in its own unit. They are very well organized trips, even to the carrying of mechanics and spare parts. It's like being on a well-run cruise.

In some ways this type of travel isn't too different from travel in Captain Marcy's time, back in 1859. One of the first things he talks about in his journal is the organization of the wagon train:

> The first business is to organize a company and elect a commander. The company should be of sufficient magnitude to herd and guard animals, and for protection against Indians. The commander's duties should be to direct the order of march, the time of starting and halting, to select the camps, detail and give orders to guards, and, indeed, to control and superintend all the movements of the company. . . .
>
> On such a journey, there is much to interest and amuse one who is fond of picturesque scenery, and of wild life in its most primitive aspects, yet no one should attempt it without anticipating many rough knocks and much hard labor; every man must expect to do his share of duty faithfully and without murmur.

Even today caravan travel appeals to a lot of people because they will be in the company of experienced personnel. Just the thought of a breakdown while alone in Mexico would keep many a family north of the border. The reasons for caravan travel are not too different today from what they were 100 years ago. Marcy's *Prairie Traveler* told all that had to be known to make the trip in those days. Today's caravan organizers do a similar job for you.

When the early travelers went across the country seeking land it was there for the taking. It dwindled fast with the increase of the western migration. In many ways, a similar thing is happening today to the RV population. By 1980 it's estimated that there will be more than three million mobile living units on the road, almost a million of which will be motor homes. This is going to put a burden on the land. Although the public land is for public use, the legislators won't stand for cutting it up for campers. As more and more private investors enter the campground business they, too, will object to the use of public lands for campgrounds. As they become stronger they will lobby to protect their investments. The motel interests in some areas have already lobbied against the free overnight sleeping in rest areas along the roads. The problem the campsite owner faces is that land values and taxes in attractive areas are so high and the camping season is so short that the investment is shaky. The private campgrounds must have a high occupancy rate.

The first motels in this country were nothing more than little cabins scattered around on a lawn. Today they are quite luxurious. The first campgrounds were nothing more than cleared sites; today people want facilities and services.

CONDOMINIUM CAMPGROUNDS

Here is a concept that has a big future. Condominium campsites are already successful. A number of land development companies are watching the leader in this field, Venture Out, and are getting geared to move in. Venture Out started in Gatlinburg, Tennessee, a rustic mountain resort in the Great Smokies. They built a luxury resort—heated swimming pools, tile bath-houses, recreation halls with planned activities, stores, laundries. All the hook-up utilities

An RV condominium on the water

are underground. The whole area is landscaped and not a trash can can be seen. You can buy your own campsite for about four thousand dollars. Each space is about thirty by sixty feet and has all the necessary hook-ups. It will always be there for you when you arrive. If you want, you can have it rented out when you are not using it. The management will split the fee of five dollars a night with you. This income could easily offset the monthly condominium fee of ten to fifteen dollars for maintenance.

Venture Out has moved into different areas of the country to establish condominiums with a wide variety of resort living—beaches in Florida, the wide-open spaces of Arizona, or the mountain country of Colorado.

Outdoor Resorts of America is another corporation setting up a major chain of RV resorts. They have 1450 sites on Nettles Island, thirty miles north of Palm Beach, Florida, and expect to spend $5,000,000. This is only the first of fifteen resort areas they plan to develop.

Even some of the RV manufacturers' clubs are getting in the act to insure their own futures. Airstream owners in New York State, for example, are establishing their own condominium.

The pinch is already being felt. Public and private camping facilities are overcrowded in some areas. A decade ago campgrounds were a sideline for a few families who owned choice pieces of land or a farmer who happened to have some acreage on a lake. Today 65 percent of the 657,000 campsites in the United States are privately owned. That percentage will increase, since neither the federal government nor the states have the money or the inclination to expand further. The federal government now has 30,000 sites at 420 locations, and the states provide about 200,000, but it's still not enough. They would like to encourage the private investors.

The condominium idea is the bright spot on the horizon. This is the way you will be able to insure having the spot you want when you take your vacation. But the beauty of this living on wheels is that you won't be tied to your vacation spot. The investment in the condominium will appreciate; rentals will help pay the carrying charges and you can still take your trips throughout the year to other places that interest you.

Some day the sociologists will investigate the impact of trailers, campers, mini-motor homes, and motor homes on our society. I can't guess, nor should I, what their findings will be. A child fifty years ago seldom left the confines of his own neighborhood. Today's children are being diapered at sixty miles per hour on interstate highways. One conclusion we can reach without a scientific study . . . it's better than staying home and watching TV.

What is happening to the retired RV couples on the interstate highways? Interviews with them disclose that they are not bored people. They enjoy the nomadic life and their new-found freedom.

Most people dream of that day when they can roll over in bed to catch another forty winks, skip the routine and tensions of the daily job, have a leisurely cup of coffee at 11 A.M., and do as they wish. Travel is usually a part of that dream. The recreation vehicle can make that dream come true. Many retired couples are traveling with the sun—Canada in the summer and warmer climates in the winter. But it's not that simple; it's not as free and easy as the TV commercials depict it to be. The simple fact of not having a permanent address can cause problems.

213

MAIL . . . PLEASE FORWARD

While you are sitting at the beach and the snow is piling up at home, the mail still has to get through. Temporary absence from an address can be handled by a neighbor or a member of the family or the mail can be held at the post office for your return. For the family who are picking up stakes, there are a number of alternatives for handling the mail. The address can be changed to that of a friend or relative who will agree to send it on. First-class mail is forwarded at no extra cost; other mail has to be paid for at the original rate. Magazines are expensive to send on because the publisher ships under a bulk rate which is not passed on for forwarding.

For those who have no one to handle mail for them, arrangements can be made with the post office to forward the mail. A forwarding form is made out at your local post office. The mail will be sent on to the new address. When you leave that address a form must be sent back to the original office to show the new forwarding address. A similar change-of-address card should be made out for the post office you are about to leave so that any mail in transit will be sent on. You should not try to have your mail catch up with you on short stopovers. Your new address would be to a specific post office—"General Delivery, hold for arrival." Mail will be held in General Delivery for ten days, then it must be returned. So in this respect, you have to plan ahead.

If you have been staying at your condominium or at a campground that has been your address, the management can handle forwarding the mail to you when you move on.

In major metropolitan areas there are companies which act as mail forwarders. Banks are also starting to enter this field and for a fee they will handle the mail problem. The customer-service agent of your local post-office system will know who these forwarding agents are. In such arrangements, your address will be in care of the forwarding agent.

Banking is not too difficult a problem for the RVers who are retiring to this life. When you start off you should retain the bank you have been doing business with. Later, if you settle, you can switch to a bank in the new locale.

You should arrange for an American Express card and at least one other bank card, such as Master Charge or BankAmericard.

Arrangements should be made for any incoming checks to be mailed by the sender directly to your bank for deposit into your account. This applies to pensions, dividends, rents, royalties, social security, and so on.

There are a number of ways to draw money out of your account while traveling. With the American Express card, you can go to any of their offices and cash a personal check for up to $250 in either traveler's checks or cash. Of course traveler's checks are the safest way to carry money.

It's not easy to walk into a strange bank and cash a check. The bank credit card eliminates this embarrassment. You can go to a member bank of your particular credit card system and get a cash advance for any amount up to your credit line. The usual minimum of credit is $500. It'll take an hour or so for a bank anywhere in the continental United States to confirm through the computer center what your credit balance is. You will receive the money upon confirmation. Then you should immediately send a check from your account by mail to your bank and have it deposited into your credit card account. The cash advance is not the same as a merchandise purchase in a store. Interest on a store purchase does not begin until twenty-five days after the billing date. Interest on a credit-card cash advance starts as soon as the paperwork reaches your bank. If your check gets there at about the same time as the paperwork does you won't have much in the way of interest charges to pay.

Large sums of money can be handled by instructing your home bank by letter to wire money to you via a local bank. You can collect this money by showing proper identification.

Any deposits you wish to make can of course be sent in by mail in the usual manner. The big trick is to have enough cash to send to the bank in the first place.

A NEW KIND OF ADDRESS

We have interviewed families who have chucked the ways of the world and are now living in either large trailers or motor homes. When they get tired of one place they move on to the next. They usually team up with other couples who live the same life, and friendships develop since they have so much in common.

When one retired couple was asked about the cost of this type of life, they put it in very simple terms. They said that the taxes alone that they had paid on their house each year more than paid for the hook-ups they had to rent. They no longer needed the big house, so they sold it. They spent a certain amount of time with their children who were scattered in different parts of the country. Before their stays became too long, they would be off on their own again. The one thing they could not see was staying put in their home and spending the working part of each day dillydallying around and doing maintenance. Food costs were about the same whether they cooked it on a foundation or on wheels, but the home owners' and property insurance they saved each year paid for at least three months' worth of food.

The money they'd received for their house more than paid for their new and bigger motor home and they had money left over to invest after they bought their condominium. They felt that they could manage very nicely within their budget.

Another couple had much the same story, except they had kept their home and traveled six to eight months a year. They enjoyed the freedom of their nomadic life but at the same time they could not give up their house. The wife explained it by saying that she had always had a fixed place . . . a house to go to. Yes, she enjoyed their motor home, but after a half-year or more she wanted more space. When spring came she wanted to start a garden and putter around. They had learned through all their traveling that it was

216

not the particular house near Boston that she needed, but they kept it because it was the one they had.

Questioning this lady further revealed another aspect of her feelings. It was psychological: stated in simple terms, a permanent address gave her a sense of security, a sense of belonging. An address was important.

A NEW CONCEPT . . . AN RV HOUSE

The discussion with our lady from near Boston started the wheels of innovation moving. We have talked to as many RVers as we could about the idea of combining a motor home and a house. Our innovation would be a union of the best and most important features of two ways of life.

But let's go back and start at the beginning. As we said earlier, the family structure has changed in this country. The concept of the family homestead is a thing of the past. Young people are not marrying the boy or girl from down the street or from the farm three miles up the road. Sometimes they're not even marrying—but that's another book.

Family structure isn't the only area of life where changes are taking place; the whole concept of work has changed in the past two decades. No longer does a man plan to work until he drops over. Retirement once was only for the rich; now it's in the cards for every man, whether he likes it or not. No one quite believed it in the 1930s when Social Security started, but it did come to pass.

Middle-class America is retiring in all sorts of ways. The aim is to get away from the fast pace our society has set up for itself, to get out from under the heavy tax burden and to find a little peace and quiet in the sun.

Recognizing people's needs for a permanent address and a place they can call home has given me an idea that will satisfy the desire for both roots and mobility—it's called the Combination Home. It can be built on a piece of land of the owner's choice—in the solitude of the countryside, as some people want, or it can fit into the condominium scheme of real-estate development.

1 RECREATION VEHICLE

2 GARAGE

3 TOOL SHED &

4 UTILITY ROOM (*HEATER · AIR COND'T'R FREEZER · WASHER · DRY'R*)

5 CLOSET · STORAGE

6 WORKROOM · DEN

7 SLIDING WALL (*TO ADJUST TO VEHICLE DOOR*)

8 MAIN ROOM

9 CLOSET

10 FIREPLACE

11 HIDE-A-BED

12 BAR (*DIVIDER*)

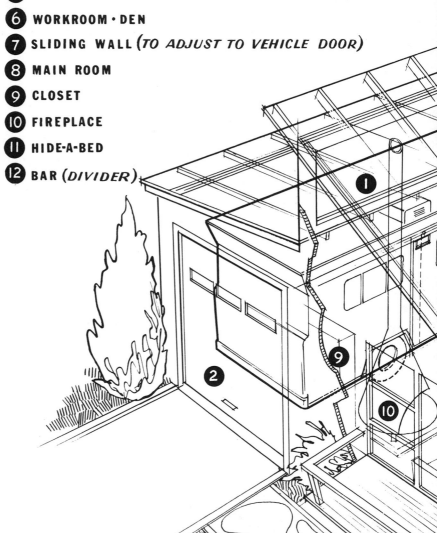

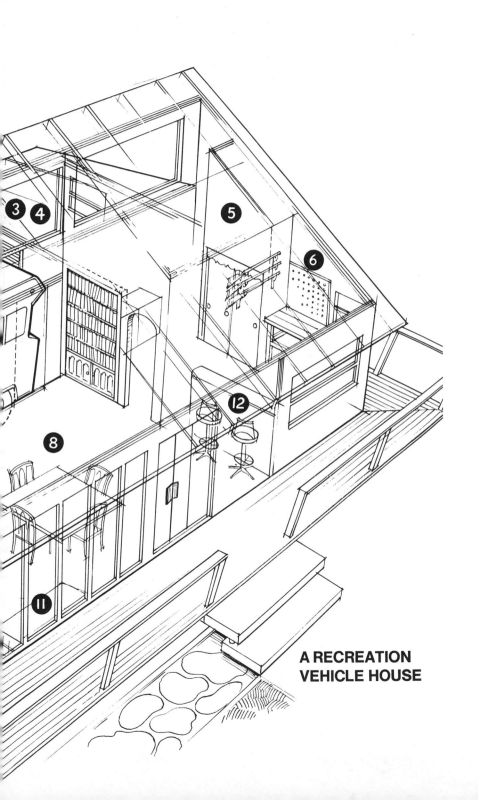

**A RECREATION
VEHICLE HOUSE**

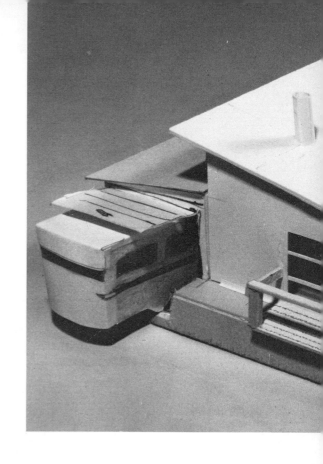

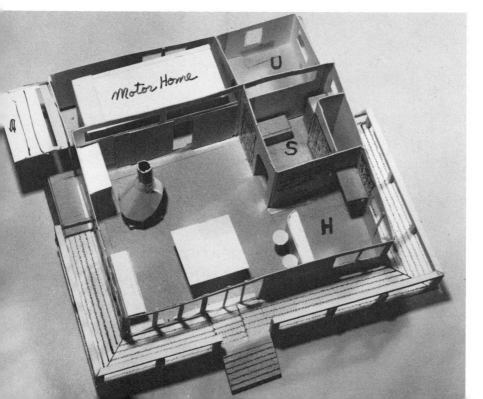

When artist Bill Bartlett finished his drawing on the preceding pages, we constructed a fast cardboard model to see how the spaces worked out in three dimensions. An outside view *(top)*, with the motor home going into the garage, shows the overall look and proportions. Left photo, with the roof removed, shows the spaces for work, play and living. The storage room (S) could be a future bathroom; the hobby area (H) could become a kitchen; the utility (U) could have a workshop. The rear view of the RV house *(right)* shows the use of high windows to give maximum light. The motor home still provides the sleeping, bathroom and cooking facilities.

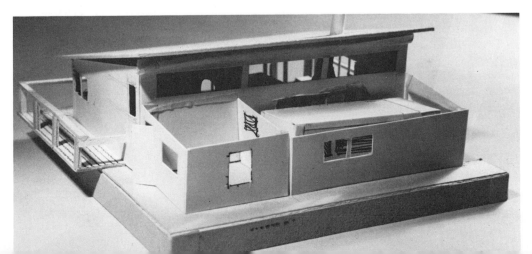

The combination house would be basically a one-room structure. It would be divided into two main areas, a garage for the recreation vehicle and a large living area. The plan would work for either a trailer or a motor home. The motor home would be driven right into the garage; a trailer could be winched in. The garage area would be separated from the living area by a sliding wall. This wall could be constructed to work in much the same fashion as do leaves on an expanding table. One section would be a doorway. It would be set anywhere in the wall. The purpose of the removable wall sections is to be able to put the doorway into the living area opposite the door of the motor home. This way it can fit any RV unit. The floor of the garage would be lower than the floor of the living area. Then the floor of the motor home and the living room would be on the same level.

What would be needed in such a house? Bedrooms would not be necessary since you already have sleeping quarters in the RV. Convertible couches could be built into the house living area. This then could function as a guest room if needed. A fine kitchen already exists in the RV, so there is no need to duplicate it. A bathroom in the house might be good, but it's not essential. The bathroom in the RV can be hooked up directly to a septic tank, and a lot of building costs will be cut. When the house is built, plumbing could be installed for the future installation of a bathroom.

Air-conditioning and heat will be necessary. If we assume that such a house will be erected in the warmer climes, a heat pump (a combination furnace and air-conditioner) will do both jobs very nicely. Both areas of the house will be heated or cooled. The RV will be in the house environment.

A combination storage and utility room has to be in the plan. Here is where you'll have the hot-water heater, clothes washer and dryer, small freezer, and a storage space for all the odds and ends that we all seem to collect.

What are the dimensions of such a structure? The height and length of the longest motor home will determine the minimums for two of the measurements. A structure 11 feet high and 30 × 30 feet would give a living area of 30 × 20. That's a lot of spread-out area.

220

What else is needed? A dining area. It could be of the fold-away-table type. A social area could be centered around a freestanding fireplace, which works well and is inexpensive. A work area, whether it be for sewing, tying flies, or whatever, could easily be worked in. Add to that lots of glass on three sides, with plenty of cabinet space below the windows. A no-maintenance deck around three sides would make for good inside-outside living.

The detailing of the truck-type garage door, clothes-closet space, outside utility storage, and other incidentals for making the space most useful can readily be worked out for each family by an architect. I've outlined the basic concept of the combination house. Its architectural form could follow one of a hundred designs. An attractive roof design, for example, can keep the structure from having the boxlike look of the mobile home.

With today's building materials, such a combination home will present little or no maintenance problems. There are a multitude of materials from which an architect can choose. There is no reason, either, why such a house could not be prefabricated and erected on a concrete slab. If the ingenious use of space that the recreation-vehicle industry has learned were applied to a house, it would make for very simple but excellent living.

How would it all work? Not too differently from moving to an apartment after spending many years in a house. You still would have a permanent address, a place where you belong. But there would be the flexibility of opening the garage door, unhooking the motor home, and driving off. The milk and mail delivery would be stopped, and you'd go down the road.

DRIVING

If driving a recreation vehicle is a new experience, here are some tips.

Most people are accustomed to the automobile and are used to its response. To graduate up to an RV should not be a frightening prospect, but it will take some rethinking.

When you walk toward your parked unit you should make note of your exact situation in relationship to other parked vehicles or other objects that are in your path, front and rear. A small car parked close behind a motor home may not be seen by the driver once he is in his driver's seat. Some car drivers have the habit of leaving a parking spot by backing until they touch the bumper of the car behind them. This will cause damage if you do it with a motor home.

Take some tips from bus drivers. They travel at all times with their headlights on. It has been proven that headlights, even in the daytime, make a vehicle more visible.

Because trucks, buses, and motor homes place the driver relatively high, there are some blind spots along the sides of the vehicle. These can be eliminated by using convex mirrors in conjunction with the truck-type side mirrors. Be cautious of the small car in the right-hand lane of a super-highway traveling abreast of your front bumper. He is hard to see, especially in the daytime. Don't pull back into a right-hand lane until you are sure this area is clear. At night you will see his headlights on the road ahead.

Some drivers have a habit of swinging the steering wheel back and forth a few inches. They are constantly overcorrecting. This is a bad habit, especially in vehicles with power steering. In a heavy RV unit, or with a trailer, this sets up an oscillation that can cause loss of control. The best position for placing the hands on a steering wheel is the one racing-car drivers use—the hands at the ten and two o'clock positions on the wheel. Make every motion a steady one.

Power brakes should be pumped, not jammed on. Locking the brakes can lead into a skid. It is false to think that the extra traction of the dual wheels or the heavy weight of the vehicle will prevent skidding. Allow plenty of room to stop. Make a road test and learn to judge the distance needed to halt the vehicle at different speeds. Add something to that distance in rain or snow conditions. The heavier the vehicle, the greater distance it takes to stop it.

If you do get into a skid, do not use the brake. It will increase the sideways momentum. A skid must be caught in the first second or so. Recovery is then easy: steer the vehicle in the direction in which the rear end is skidding. Do not feed gas in an attempt to power the vehicle back into the lane. This can turn a mild skid into a spin.

On the road your height at the wheel gives you excellent visibility ahead. Take advantage of it; anticipate what the traffic is doing. This gives you extra time to slow down or change lanes if need be.

Take all curves much more slowly than in a car. Curves, especially on downhill grades, can cause problems. Centrifugal force can swing you to the outside of a curve or out of your lane. Play it safe and reduce speed. Stay to the right when going uphill and let the faster traffic pass.

Reduce your speed in gusty winds. At high speed, the wind can throw you out of your lane. The wind pressure of a fast passing bus or truck can produce the same result. Hold the wheel steady! Do not overcorrect. A large truck at high speed produces heavy turbulence. Don't ride too close behind him; drop back and avoid the buffeting of that turbulence.

NIGHT DRIVING

Make sure all your running lights and signal lights are in working order and that windows and mirrors are clean. Although cars can tell when they are clear of you when they pass, longer rigs have a more difficult time making this judgment. When the passing vehicle has cleared you and has room to pull over to the right, flash your high beams high, then low. That's the trucker's signal that it is safe to pull back into the right lane.

Be sure to use the night-driving curtain behind you if lights are going to be used in the living quarters of the motor home. Reflections on the windshield can be very confusing. It's wise on long trips, especially at night, to change position often.

Night speeds should be slower than daylight speeds. Know where you are going ahead of time; the driver should never try to figure out the road map while underway.

Branches of trees that a car can pass under can do damage to the sides of a motor home or trailer; so on narrow country roads, be very careful and reduce speed. If you stay in your lane, you won't have tree problems, because road crews keep branches trimmed for the truck traffic. Stay out of the center of the road while avoiding tree limbs; you might not be avoiding oncoming traffic.

Know your vehicle's exact height in feet and inches, and be sure to read the warning signs posted before you come to an underpass. Before entering a garage, make sure the person who is guiding you in knows if you have some extension on top, as he won't be able to see roof vents or air-conditioners from the ground.

Do not hog space in a gas station. Move your rig to the forward pump so others can get gas. Make sure you clear canopies or lighting fixtures at the pumps.

If you are traveling in convoy with other motor homes or trailers, leave enough space between the units so the faster traffic can pass without any problem.

If you are trailering, get to know your length. When passing a vehicle, make sure you have plenty of clearance before pulling back into the right-hand lane.

There is a trick to backing vehicles in tow. Place your hand at the bottom of the steering wheel, then move the hand and wheel in the direction you want the towed vehicle to go. Once it's moving in the right direction, hold the wheel steady. Never cut the wheels hard when backing up.

CHANGING A TIRE

If a dual tire blows you can go very slowly to a station to have it changed. It's good to stop frequently to check whether the flat tire is getting hot. At high speed it could catch fire. If a tire has to be changed on the road, move to the shoulder. Set out flares and station someone to direct traffic. Use only a hydraulic jack on a heavy vehicle. Carry a quarter-inch steel plate to set the jack on so the small base of the jack won't dig into a soft road shoulder and fall over.

Set the hand brake. Put the engine in gear. Block the tires with rocks. If possible do the whole operation on a level spot. Set the jack on the steel plate and line it up under the axle. Raise it until it's set. Unloosen the lugs before the tire is raised. Raise the tire and remove the lugs. Keep out from under the vehicle when the tire is off. If it's a rear tire, the body of the vehicle may have to be raised to get the tire out of the tire well. Use a car bumper jack to lift the body high enough off the springs to clear the removal of the tire. Replace the tire and put the lugs on. Remember lugs are left-hand threads. Put all the lugs on hand-tight. Then tighten opposite lugs in rotation. Check the manual instructions; some dual rims have a pin to align. Make the lugs as tight as possible.

No one should be in the vehicle when a tire is being changed. Never get into a position when under the vehicle where you would be pinned if the jack slipped. Keep children away while doing the job.

WINTER STORAGE

If you do not plan to use the vehicle for an extended period there are several procedures that should be followed.

Remove all fresh water. Drain the main tanks and open the valves in all the lines. Open the faucets. Close all faucets and valves when the water is drained, and pressurize the system. The best way to do this is with your built-in air pump. With the pressure up to normal, open the faucet at the farthest end of the line and allow the air to bleed off and carry the water with it. When no more water comes out with the air, the system is clear. Check this out by re-pressurizing and opening other valves in the system.

Clear and clean all holding tanks. Flush them out. Drain the toilet, following the manufacturer's recommendations. Deodorize the system and leave the toilet gate valve closed.

Close the LP gas valves. Close all roof vents and windows.

Clean the entire interior. Remove fishing gear and foodstuffs, as they will cause odors. Remove medicines and any bottled goods that could freeze. Clean the air-conditioner filter. Seal all vent openings with tape to prevent birds and animals from nesting inside compartments.

Winterize the automotive system according to the manufacturer's recommendations. Be sure the tires are inflated correctly. For long storage put the unit on blocks if possible. Remove the batteries and keep them in a warm place.

THE SPRING GET-READY

Those warm, sunny spring days tell you it's time to get the motor home ready for the road. Flush out the fresh-water system and give it a Clorox treatment. Check all faucet washers; winter storage sometimes hardens them. Check the windows; they may need a treatment with Slipit or penetrating oil. Remove all winter vent covers and check all compartments for obstructions or flammable materials. Check and run all appliances. Be sure the pilot lights are burning with a full flame. Check the complete electrical systems. Give the complete liquid propane system a check-over using the soap solution method.

Check the automotive manual and follow any special instructions. Replace the batteries and see that the connections are clean and tight. Check the tires for pressure, a thing that should be done in all seasons. Give the vehicle a spin and check the steering, brakes, and driving response. Check out automotive electrical systems and all running lights.

A FEW EXTRA MAINTENANCE TIPS

Spots and Stains should be removed immediately. Carry a good upholstery cleaner. Work from the outside of a stain toward the center. Change the cleaning cloth often. When the spot is removed, wipe the area briskly with a clean absorbent towel and allow to dry. Never use bleach, laundry soap, gasoline, or lacquer thinner on carpeting or fabric. They can cause damage. Lipstick, ink, grease, and mustard may be impossible to remove. Candy, shoe polish, oil, butter, and tar can be removed with cleaning fluid. Coffee, soft drinks, ice cream, catsup, milk, and blood should be soaked with cold water before using a fabric cleaner.

Tips: if you are going to have a workman inside the unit, take up the rug if you can; if you can't, put paper down or have him take off his shoes.

Sink. Stainless steel can be pitted by salt, mustard, and mayonnaise. Clean away such items immediately. A mild detergent will handle normal cleaning. Rinse with warm water and wipe dry to avoid streaks. A mild abrasive will clean stubborn stains. Work in the direction of the polish. To keep the original finish, polish with a wax cleaner and rub with a soft cloth.

Stove. After it's cool the stove can be cleaned with soap and water. The oven racks and broiler pan can be removed and washed in the sink. Stubborn spots can be cleaned off with baking soda and oven cleaner.

The stove vent-fan has a filter that should be cleaned periodically. Remove the filter and soak it in a detergent solution. Shake it dry and replace it.

Refrigerator. Never use a strong abrasive on the refrigerator shelves. A mild detergent solution will do the job. The freezing compartment and ice trays should be cleaned only in hot water. When the refrigerator is not being used, leave the door ajar. Never leave any food in the refrigerator or anywhere in the RV when it's not in use.

Walls and ceiling. Do not saturate the walls or ceiling with water when cleaning. A damp cloth and mild detergent will do the job best. The paneling can be cleaned with.a wood and wax cleaner. The Fiberglas walls of the bathroom should be cleaned with a mild detergent, and then a cleaning wax will help retain the original luster. The floor can be cleaned with a mild abrasive cleaner or detergent. The toilet bowl should be cleaned with a nonabrasive cleaner. Strong chemicals may damage the seal or the finish of the bowl.

Tip: carry a jar of Vaseline and periodically coat the ball that seals the toilet. Work the lever back and forth as the grease is applied. This is usually necessary after long periods of storage.

Exterior care. Wash the exterior frequently with warm water and detergent. A long-handled car-washing brush will enable you to reach all areas. This will prevent surface damage from calcium chloride and road salts. Clean off road tars and tree saps with a mild solvent. Never wash or wax in the direct rays of the sun. Apply a heavy wax finish especially to the front of the unit, as previously mentioned; it'll make bug removal easier. A nylon net-covered sponge soaked in detergent is the best way to remove bugs. Never use strong solvents or abrasives.

Tip: hang a piece of aluminum screening in front of the automotive radiator. Catch the bugs on it instead of allowing them to clog the radiator. Brush it periodically.

Once a year, check all exterior roof joints; resealing with silicone sealant may be necessary. Carry wide cloth tape for temporary repairs to the exterior wall; it will protect the interior wall from the weather.

Periodically check for chassis rust. Use a wire brush on rusted areas and paint with undercoat or rust-resistant paint.

As the seasons change you may want to carry different items. Here is a list to start you off:

Extra fire extinguisher
Flashlights
Road flares
Tow chain
Hand winch
Hand tools
Hose and hose "Y"
No. 12 extension cord
Extension light
Extension connectors
Small ax
Infra-red bulb (winter)
Snow shovel (winter)
Electric heater (winter)
Tire gauge (long shank for duals)
Fuses
First-aid kit
Leveling boards
Metal plate to put under hydraulic jack
Baling wire
Wooden bat for testing the tires by sound
Extra flints for the refrigerator starter
Cloth tape
Extra oil and funnel for electric generator
Grease rags
Nylon-covered sponge

Get a list from your automotive dealer of small parts that are difficult to obtain—fan belt, points, and so on.

DO'S AND DON'TS

DO'S:

Walk around the vehicle every time you stop just to check that all is in order. Don't forget the spare tire.

Remember to put up the step before you start.

Make sure the door is locked before you move.

Check to see that the stove is off and no pots are sitting on it.

Check that all objects are battened down before moving.

Be sure all seat belts are fastened before you start moving.

Be sure all occupants let the driver know before they get up and move about.

Be sure the driver lets everyone know when he's about to move.

Provide a boat gimbal for the driver's coffee. It could prevent an accident.

Always apply the accelerator in a steady manner, especially when going uphill in snow or rain.

Keep your running lights on and remember your extra length if you are towing.

Keep the back window clean; it's important to your visibility.

Carry an extra set of keys.

DON'TS:

Don't drive off roads unnecessarily. Bumps and torque could cause structural problems.

Don't overload the vehicle. Keep heavy things at low levels.

Dump the holding tank only at a dumping station.

Never use the dumping station hose to take on fresh water.

Think of the other fellow; he's on his vacation too. When arriving in a campground at night, your headlights are going to annoy those already asleep. Lights played on a tent light up the whole inside. Keep your voices down and make as little noise as possible. Remember, you'll want to talk to your neighbor in the morning. Don't slam doors or start chopping wood at midnight.

If you have pets, don't let them become a pest to someone else; clean up after them.

If you are not using a drain hook-up, use a plastic bucket to catch your dirty water. Dispose of it where it won't interfere with others.

If someone has set out an object, such as a chair, it's a signal that they are coming back and that it's their campsite. Honor their staked-out claim.

Enjoy seeing the wildlife but don't interfere with the animals or feed them, for their safety and yours. Do not leave food outside at night.

Others will follow you, so don't destroy the trees or bushes.

Anyplace is a good place to practice the Golden Rule, so leave your campsite cleaner than you found it.

You are an ambassador for the sport of recreation-vehicle living. Act accordingly.

INDEX

INDEX